AF413585

AN EPIC GUIDE TO GO INTO DEPRESSION

ASHISH CECIL MURMU

INDIA • SINGAPORE • MALAYSIA

Dedicated to

"Misery"

*Thanks for always being there, even when
I wanted you to leave.*

Contents

Contents

"The Masterclass You Never Knew You Needed"

Welcome to the preface of *"An Epic Guide to Go into Depression,"* a masterclass in transforming your life into a veritable festival of gloom. If you're reading this, chances are you're either a connoisseur of dark humour, someone who appreciates the finer points of sarcasm, or you're genuinely curious about how to turn your life's lemons into a bitter, undrinkable concoction of despair. Regardless of your reason, you're in for a treat. Or a trick. Depends on your perspective.

Have you ever wondered why self-help books are always so nauseatingly positive? With their endless mantras of *"You can do it!"* and *"Believe in yourself!"* they paint a picture of life that's almost offensively upbeat. Well, we're here to rectify that. This book isn't about lifting you up; it's about dragging you down with a smile on your face. It's about embracing the suck with a sense of humour and a keen understanding of the absurdities of life.

"An Epic Guide to Go into Depression" is an anti-self-help book. It's a hilarious, biting, and honest look at all the ways we unwittingly sabotage our own happiness. It's for those who are tired of the relentless optimism and want to explore the darker, funnier side of human nature. This book is not about finding the light at the end of the tunnel; it's about setting up camp in the middle of the tunnel and making the best of the darkness.

The journey to write this book began when I realized that the path to self-destruction is often paved with good intentions. We start off wanting to succeed, to be happy, and to live balanced lives, but somewhere along the way, things go hilariously wrong. Instead of becoming the best versions of ourselves, we become experts at making our lives more complicated and less fulfilling. This book is a celebration of those missteps, those comedic errors, and the perverse genius of turning small issues into full-blown crises.

Writing this book was a cathartic experience. It allowed me to laugh at my own failures and the ridiculousness of life's challenges. It's amazing how liberating it can be to admit that sometimes, life is just a series of unfortunate events strung together by moments of misguided optimism. By embracing the chaos and finding humour in the darkness, I discovered that there's a peculiar kind of freedom in acknowledging that things are not always going to go right — and that's perfectly okay.

This book is divided into chapters that cover every conceivable way to invite misery into your life. From the subtle art of *Denying Your Emotions* to the sophisticated techniques of *Surrounding Yourself with Toxic People,* each chapter is a deep dive into the habits and mindsets that can turn a perfectly good life into a melodramatic soap opera. You'll learn how to perfect the *Work-Life Imbalance,* master the skill of *Self-Criticism,* and avoid *Exercise* like a pro. And let's not forget the joys of *Holding Grudges and Living in the Past* — both essential skills for anyone serious about cultivating a life of woe.

In crafting this guide book, I drew inspiration from history, literature, and the everyday absurdities of modern life. From the tragic heroes of Greek mythology who taught us the value of *hubris* to the bureaucratic nightmares of contemporary office culture, this book pulls from a wide array of sources to illustrate just how universal the pursuit of unhappiness can be. The goal is not just to make you laugh but to make you think — and maybe even help you see the lighter side of your darkest moments.

I hope you find this book as entertaining to read as it was to write. It's a labour of love, crafted with the intention of offering a new perspective on the age-old quest for happiness. Instead of telling you how to be happy, this book shows you how absurdly easy it is to be unhappy, often through our own misguided efforts.

So, sit back, relax, and prepare to dive into the most entertaining guide to depression you'll ever read. Remember, if you're going to be miserable, you might as well do it with a sense of humour. Welcome to *"An Epic Guide to Go into Depression."* Let the journey begin!

***

"Welcome to Your Epic Journey"

Welcome, dear reader, to *"An Epic Guide to Go into Depression,"* the ultimate manual for those who aspire to transform their otherwise mundane existence into a masterpiece of melancholia. This book is not just any guide; it's a comprehensive, witty, and sarcastic blueprint designed to help you navigate the labyrinth of life's miseries with finesse and flair. Prepare yourself for an epic journey, one filled with dark humour, biting sarcasm, and a healthy dose of reality. Whether you're here out of sheer curiosity, genuine need, or simply a love for gallows humour, this book promises to deliver an unforgettable experience.

Imagine, if you will, a world where everything that can go wrong does so in the most spectacular fashion. Picture yourself as the protagonist in this tragicomedy, navigating the pitfalls and pratfalls of daily life with the grace of a three-legged elephant. This is the world we will explore together, a world where Murphy's Law is not just a rule but a way of life. In this journey, we'll cover every possible way to sabotage your happiness, from denying your emotions to surrounding yourself with the most toxic people imaginable.

Let's begin with a fundamental truth: life is hard, and it's even harder when you're determined to make it so. Why strive for contentment when you can wallow in misery? Why seek balance when you can teeter on the brink of despair? This book is for those who believe that if something is worth doing, it's worth overdoing — especially when it comes to self-sabotage.

Our first chapter, *"Denying Your Emotions,"* will teach you to treat your feelings like that obnoxious relative who never takes a hint and always overstays their welcome. Why confront your emotions when you can bottle them up until they explode and cause maximum chaos? After all, who needs therapists when you can be a Victorian ghost — repressed and in denial?

Next up, we delve into the fine art of *"Surrounding Yourself with Toxic People."* Think of your life as a botanical garden. Now, instead of nurturing beautiful flowers, fill it with weeds, poisonous vines, and a few hungry Venus flytraps. Toxic people are the energy vampires who transform every day into an episode of a melodramatic soap opera. Embrace them, adore them, and let them drag you down to new depths of woe.

In the *"Work-Life Imbalance"* chapter, we'll show you how to let your job completely consume your existence. Who needs hobbies, friends, or family when you can spend every waking minute chasing deadlines and cowering before your inbox? Modern work culture glorifies the grind, so sacrifice your well-being on the altar of productivity. Remember, sleep is for the weak, and vacations are for those with *"less important"* jobs.

Self-criticism is an art form we'll perfect together. Learn how to beat yourself up with the precision of a seasoned martial artist. Achieved something great? Clearly, it's because nobody else wanted the job. Received a compliment? They were probably just being polite. By the end of this chapter, you'll be a black belt in self-deprecation.

"Exercise: How to Avoid It" is your guide to maintaining a sedentary lifestyle for peak misery. Who needs endorphins when you can binge on Netflix and junk food? Exercise is for those who enjoy feeling alive. For the true connoisseur of gloom, the couch is your throne, and the remote is your sceptre. Forget the gym; the only lifting you need is of your spirits — with a side of ice cream.

Mastering *"Isolation and Loneliness"* is crucial for anyone truly committed to their depression journey. Perfect loneliness in a crowd with advanced skill. Become a hermit in the digital age, avoiding real social interactions whenever possible. Texting is safer than talking, and social media is a splendid substitute for actual human contact. Why bother with messy relationships when you can curate your interactions from the safety of your screen?

In *"The Perfectionist's Playbook,"* we'll teach you to set impossibly high standards and then mercilessly berate yourself for not meeting them. Aim for the stars, and when you fall short, ensure you beat yourself up thoroughly. Perfectionism is the gift that keeps on giving — mostly in the form of chronic stress and a perpetual sense of inadequacy.

"The Financial Fiasco" chapter will guide you to ensure that financial troubles weigh you down. Who needs stability when you can drown in debt, squander your cash, and avoid budgeting like the plague? Financial freedom is overrated; financial chaos is where the real excitement lies.

"Social Media: The Comparison Trap" will show you how to make your life feel pathetically insignificant by comparing it to others. Scroll through curated snapshots of others' seemingly perfect lives and convince yourself you're failing miserably. Social media isn't just a platform; it's a tool for self-inflicted psychological torment.

"Holding Grudges and Not Letting Go" is an art you can perfect with practice. Harbor resentment forever and let it fester until it consumes you. Forgiveness is for saints and saps; cling to your grudges like they're precious heirlooms.

In *"Living in the Past,"* we'll explore how to replay your mistakes and regrets on a continuous loop for an exquisite dive into sorrow. Nostalgia is a comforting prison where you're both the warden and the inmate.

"Neglecting Hobbies and Passions" will teach you how to forsake what brings you joy. Why bother with hobbies when you can focus solely on work? Hobbies are for those with spare time, and passions are mere distractions from real responsibilities.

"The Power of Negative Thinking" will explore how to embrace pessimism as your shield and sword, protecting you from disappointment while shielding you from hope. Optimism is for the naïve.

In *"The Science of Overthinking,"* we'll turn minor issues into grand crises. Overthinking is like a mental gym; the more you practice, the stronger your anxiety muscles become. Simple decisions turn into complex puzzles, and every action is fraught with potential disaster.

"The Diet of Despair" will show you how to eat your way into a depressive state. Comfort food is the only true comfort, and nutrition is a myth. Indulge in sugar, fat, and regret for the ultimate indulgence.

"Avoiding Professional Help" ensures you never get better. Therapy is for the mentally weak, and medication is just a crutch. Embrace your suffering and wear it as a badge of honour.

"Unhealthy Relationships" will show you how to fill your life with drama and toxicity. Relationships should be chaotic and emotionally draining. Stability is for the boring.

"Procrastination: The Ultimate Sabotage" will teach you to put off happiness one task at a time. Procrastination is the thief of time and the destroyer of dreams.

Finally, our Conclusion will summarize the book's insights and offer a glimmer of hope. Even in the darkest times, there's a way out. Embrace the absurdity of life, laugh at your mistakes, and remember that you hold the power to change your narrative. The first step out of the darkness is realizing you're in it, and the next is choosing to step toward the light.

So, buckle up and prepare for an epic journey through the darkest corners of the human psyche. This guide is your ticket to a masterclass in misery, a symphony of sorrow, and a comedic exploration of despair. Welcome to *"An Epic Guide to Go into Depression"* — where laughter and tears go hand in hand.

***

Chapter 1

"Denying Your Emotions"

Welcome to the first and most essential step in your epic journey towards depression: denying your emotions. In a world obsessed with happiness, self-care, and emotional well-being, we boldly choose to swim against the tide. Forget about those pesky therapists and self-help gurus — this book is your ticket to a life filled with perfectly orchestrated breakdowns and delightfully dramatic meltdowns. Forget a sound mind; we're here to help you skilfully destroy your inner peace.

In this chapter, we'll guide you through the finest techniques to ensure your emotions remain under lock and key. So, please sit back, unwind, and prepare to either chuckle or weep your way through our manual to become an expert in emotional denial. Welcome to your exclusive master class in denying your emotions — because why face your feelings when you can suppress them and enjoy the chaos?

The Bottling Technique

First things first, let's dive into the timeless art of bottling up your emotions. Think of your feelings as fizzy soda. Keep shaking that bottle, and whatever you do, don't you dare release the cap. Ignore the fizzing, the pressure build-up, and the inevitable explosion. Just keep shaking. The goal here is to maintain a pristine exterior, completely unruffled by the turmoil within. Sure, you'll occasionally feel like you're on the verge of eruption, but remember: the trick is to keep everything inside until you absolutely can't anymore.

History has proven that repression always turns out brilliantly — just ask any former dictator! The result? A glorious, sticky explosion at the most inconvenient moment. So, keep shaking and never release. It's a guaranteed way to ensure your emotions create the biggest mess possible. The world will be absolutely astonished by your ability to implode spectacularly.

The Stiff Upper Lip

Next, we'll adopt the British approach to emotions — ignore them completely. This method is delightfully straightforward. You see, the British have truly mastered the art of emotional suppression. Adopt this strategy wholeheartedly. Wave away your feelings like you would an annoying mosquito. Emotional expression is so overrated. Plus, emotions are for the weak and those who don't understand the true value of a good, cold cup of tea. Don't forget to keep that stiff upper lip in place. It's all about ignoring feelings so effectively that you might forget you ever had them.

The British have nailed the stiff upper lip — no emotions, no problems. Next time you feel something — anything — immediately suppress it by pretending it doesn't exist. Treat your emotions like a bad weather forecast: you can acknowledge it's raining, but you don't have to step outside and get wet. Instead, stay indoors with your unfeeling heart and a tepid beverage. Who needs feelings when you can have a cold heart and an even colder approach to your emotions. Channel your inner British aristocrat and remember: it's far better to be emotionally distant than emotionally distraught. The British have been doing this for centuries, and look at how happy they are!

Cryonics for Feelings

Moving on, let's consider the cryonics method. Have you never heard of it? No worries, I'll fill you in. Cryonics is the brilliant concept of freezing oneself in the hope of being resurrected in the future. Now, let's apply this ingenious idea to your emotions. Freeze them solid, like those neon-coloured Popsicles from the 90s — vibrant on the outside but stone cold on the inside. Your emotions? Stick them in the metaphorical freezer. The colder, the better. When someone inquires about your feelings, just give them a frosty *"I'm fine,"* no matter the circumstances. Your heart should be as icy as a January morning.

Walt Disney is rumoured to have frozen himself, presumably to wake up in a future where he's relevant again. If it works for Walt Disney (allegedly), it'll work for you. You can do the same with your emotions. Just freeze them. This technique is perfect for those aspiring to have the emotional range of an ice sculpture. If you start to feel something thawing, quickly refreeze it with a hefty dose of reality TV or a mind-numbing scroll through social media.

This way, you can preserve your emotional distress for future generations. Who knows? Maybe in 200 years, scientists will thaw out your frozen tears and study them for their unique composition of sadness and denial.

The Stoic Philosophy

Marcus Aurelius was onto something when he advocated for the denial of emotions. Imagine diving into stoicism so completely that you become a living, breathing statue — metaphorically speaking, of course. Stoicism tells us that emotions are just irrational blips that need to be tamped down. Once you start to follow this philosophy, you'll find yourself responding to life's crises with the emotional range of a marble bust. Did your pet goldfish die? Keep that frown upside down! Stub your toe? Maintain that unreadable, indifferent façade. Feel like crying! Remind yourself that it's all part of the grand cosmic joke, and keep a straight face. Got dumped by your significant other? Think of it as an opportunity to practice your newfound emotional restraint. Friends and family will marvel at your unflappable demeanour as you navigate job losses, breakups, and global pandemics with the same calm detachment as someone ordering a sandwich.

The goal here is to achieve such emotional detachment that people start wondering if you've replaced your heart with a rock. Emotions are for the weak, after all. It's not about being heartless; it's about being heartlessly rational. Strive to reach a level of stoicism that would even make the ancient Greeks say, *"Wow, now that's impressive."*

Self-Help Book Bonfire

Ah, the self-help industry — full of optimistic advice on how to *"feel your feelings"* and *"embrace vulnerability."* Nonsense! If you come across any of these *touchy-feely self-help books,* stage a rebellion first and then gather all of them up for a bonfire. These books are obviously written by overly optimistic idealists who have no understanding of the true value of emotional suppression. Self-help books are for the weak, and you are anything but not weak. These books are your enemy and have no place in your life. Burn them all and watch the flames of your denial soar high, illuminating your path to a more miserable existence.

This act of defiance against emotional awareness is a ritualistic cleansing of all that threatens your stoic existence. This fiery ritual will symbolize your commitment to emotional suppression and your disdain for personal growth. Remember, if you never read about it, it doesn't exist. After all, what better way to prove your mastery over your emotions than by eradicating any literature suggesting otherwise?

Poker Face Mastery

Perfecting your poker face is an essential skill in the art of emotional denial. Aim for that perfect blank stare, one capable of concealing a tidal wave of suppressed tears. A blank stare is your best defense against anyone trying to peek into your emotional world. Spend quality time in front of a mirror until you can mask any trace of feeling, from the joy of a surprise party to the despair of your partner getting married to someone else. Just remember, showing feelings is for amateurs, and you're gunning for the gold medal in emotional stonewalling. When friends inevitably ask how you're doing, respond with a robotic *"I'm fine"* while maintaining your flawless poker face. After all, vulnerability is so passé.

Your goal is to become an enigma wrapped in a mystery tucked inside an emotional vacuum. Practice daily until even your own reflection starts questioning your humanity.

The Inner Volcano

Treat your emotions like Pompeii — simmering beneath the surface until they inevitably erupt and bury everything in sight. Pompeii was a thriving city until Mount Vesuvius decided to throw a tantrum. Your emotions are Vesuvius, and the world around you is Pompeii.

This technique requires meticulous management of your emotional pressure. Allow your feelings to build up over time, suppressing them with daily distractions and a rigid routine. Keep all those pesky feelings buried deep within until they inevitably explode gloriously, burying everything in sight under a thick layer of emotional lava.

The beauty of this technique lies in its inevitability; one day, the pressure will become too much, and you'll unleash a catastrophic emotional explosion that will leave everyone around you covered in the ashes of your repressed feelings. Sure, it'll cause destruction, but think of it as a dramatic flair to your life story. This method ensures maximum emotional impact with minimal effort and guarantees that your eventual breakdown will be remembered for years to come. Plus, you'll have a great historical analogy to use when explaining the inevitable fallout to your therapist (if you ever decide to see one).

Historical Repression

The Victorians, people who lived during the reign of Queen Victoria in the 19th century, knew how to handle emotions — by not handling them at all. When it came to managing emotions, they came up with a unique approach and invented fainting couches for a reason. Channel your inner Victorian by clasping your hand to your forehead and fainting dramatically if anyone tries to discuss feelings with you. You see, the Victorians were masters of emotional repression, often resorting to fainting spells at the mere hint of emotional discourse. During that era, emotional repression was an art form, and fainting was a socially acceptable way to avoid awkward conversations.

Perfect your swoon, clutching your handkerchief as you gracefully collapse onto the nearest fainting couch — or a regular sofa if you're feeling particularly modern. This will ensure that sensitive topics are swiftly avoided, and no one will dare to bring up such delicate matters in your fainting-prone presence again. Should someone attempt to broach the subject of your feelings, just announce, *"I sense a swoon approaching!"* and exit with as much flair as you can muster.

The Ticking Time Bomb

Use your emotions like a Swiss watch — impeccably precise, discreet, and eventually ticking down to a catastrophic explosion. This method requires meticulous planning and timing of your emotional outbursts for maximum impact. Keep a mental clock ticking, suppressing your feelings until the perfect moment to breakdown. The key is precision. When the time is right, let your emotions detonate in a spectacular display of pent-up rage, sorrow, or frustration, perhaps at a family gathering or during an important meeting. This ensures maximum emotional impact with minimum immediate effort. Plus, it adds an element of suspense to your daily interactions.

This method not only ensures that your emotional outbursts are memorable, but it also allows you to maintain a veneer of control until the very last second. The goal is to ensure that when you do finally implode, it's both unexpected and highly dramatic, leaving a lasting impression on everyone around you. It's the emotional equivalent of a fireworks show but with more screaming. Just be prepared for the collateral damage.

Cold War Tactics

Lastly, treat your emotions like a nuclear arsenal. Adopt mutually assured destruction as your strategy — make it clear that if anyone dares approach your feelings, there will be catastrophic consequences. Channel your inner Cold War-era strategies by stockpiling your emotional weaponry, ready to unleash it at the slightest provocation. This method creates an atmosphere of fear and respect, ensuring everyone tiptoes around you. The threat of emotional annihilation keeps everyone at arm's length, and you'll be able to maintain your emotional fortress unchallenged. It's all about that delicate balance of power where nobody really wins, but everyone loses equally. If it worked for global superpowers, it can surely handle your inner chaos.

Practical Exercises

To help you master these techniques, here are some practical exercises:

1. ***Emotional Bottling Drills***: Throughout your day, consciously bottle up any emotions you feel. Practice keeping a calm exterior even when faced with

distressing situations. Start with small incidents, like spilling coffee on your favourite shirt, and work your way up to bigger challenges, such as getting yelled at by your boss.

2. ***The Tea Test****:* Whenever you feel an emotion creeping up, immediately make yourself a cup of tea. Focus on the process of brewing and sipping, allowing the tea to wash away any traces of feelings. Keep a variety of teas on hand for different emotional crises.

3. ***Cryonics Visualization****:* Close your eyes and visualize placing each of your emotions into a cryonics chamber. Imagine them freezing solid, turning into unfeeling blocks of ice. This mental exercise will help reinforce your emotional detachment.

4. ***Stoic Journal****:* Keep a journal where you record your daily experiences, but in a completely emotionless tone. Describe events as if you were an alien observing human behaviour, devoid of any personal attachment or feeling.

5. ***Book Burning Ceremony****:* Gather any self-help books you own and have a ceremonial book burning. Make it a ritualistic event, perhaps inviting friends who also enjoy denying their emotions. Roast marshmallows over the flames of self-help advice.

6. ***Mirror Poker Face Practice****:* Spend 10 minutes each morning practicing your poker face in the mirror. Challenge yourself to maintain a blank expression no

matter what thoughts cross your mind. Progress to having someone tell you jokes while you keep your poker face intact.

7. ***Volcano Eruption Plan****:* Create a detailed plan for your emotional eruption. Choose a date, time, and location for your meltdown. Write down the triggers you'll allow to set off your eruption and rehearse the dramatic scene you'll make.

8. ***Victorian Swooning Practice****:* Perfect your fainting technique. Watch historical dramas for inspiration, and practice collapsing gracefully. Remember to always have a fainting couch or a soft surface nearby.

9. ***Emotion Time Bomb****:* Set a timer for your emotional explosions. Start with shorter intervals and gradually increase the duration you can keep your feelings bottled up. When the timer goes off, let out a dramatic but controlled outburst.

10. ***Cold War Emotional Standoff****:* Establish a set of rules for your emotional Cold War. Make it clear to friends and family that any attempt to discuss feelings will result in a severe response. Develop your arsenal of deterrent strategies, such as changing the subject or pretending not to hear.

Absolutely brilliant! With these top-notch techniques, you're well on your way to denying your emotions effectively and setting the stage for a spectacular descent into depression. The secret sauce to truly burying your feelings is unwavering consistency and dedication. Just keep those emotions tightly locked away, rock that impassive facade, and bask in the delightful ignorance that accompanies a total emotional blackout.

In our next chapter, we'll explore the equally important art of surrounding yourself with toxic people. Because, naturally, why would you opt for supportive, well-adjusted people when you can exclusively rely on a cast of charmingly dysfunctional characters? Brace yourself for more sage advice on your exhilarating journey to achieving peak depression! Stay tuned for the next dose of unparalleled guidance!

***

"Surround Yourself with Toxic People"

Welcome to Chapter 2 of your epic journey into the depths of depression. Here, we will help you with foolproof tips on how to perfectly ruin your life by handpicking the worst companions imaginable. If you've ever dreamed of turning your life into a never-ending reality TV show where the only plot twist is your escalating despair, you're in the right place. This chapter is dedicated to perfecting the art of surrounding yourself with toxic people — because what's life without a little drama, right?

Forget about tranquillity and self-improvement; it's time to embrace the parasitic charm of energy vampires, the endless theatrics of drama magnets, and the soul-sucking prowess of emotional vampires. Why bother with supportive friendships when you can have a personal entourage of frenemies, critics, and manipulators, each contributing their own unique brand of emotional mayhem? Think of this chapter as your guide to assembling a squad of negativity experts who are dedicated to ensuring your daily dose of chaos. So, buckle up and prepare to dive headfirst into a world where every interaction is a masterclass in self-sabotage. Because if you're not surrounded by toxicity, are you even trying to achieve maximum despair?

The Parasite Principle

First on the list: The Parasite. These are your friends who drain your energy faster than a smartphone at 1% with every app imaginable open. They're the ones calling you at 3 AM because they *just need to talk,* only to regale you with every riveting detail of their disastrous Tinder escapades. You get to live vicariously through their endless drama while sacrificing your own sanity. These folks are always around, demanding attention and giving you nothing but sheer exhaustion in return. They're like human black holes, sucking away your energy with every interaction. And when you try to share your own struggles, they will skilfully redirect the conversation back to themselves.

Make sure your friend group includes at least one chronic complainer. These are the people who have a problem for every solution and can turn any sunny day into a thunderstorm of negativity. Bonus points if they're also chronically indecisive because nothing says *"energy drain,"* like spending three hours deciding where to go for lunch. Cultivate friendships with people who drain your energy faster than anything else. The secret to maintaining this dynamic is to never, ever prioritize your own needs. Remember, you're here to serve the narrative of their chaotic lives, not your own. The goal here is to be perpetually exhausted, so their constant need for attention and support is perfect for sapping your life force. Why settle for tranquillity when you can have chaos? Answer every call, text, and cry for help, regardless of time or personal crisis. Your well-being is merely an afterthought!

The Drama Magnet

If you think life is boring, spice it up by attracting drama like a Hollywood celebrity for maximum depressive impact. These friends bring an endless supply of chaos, ensuring you never have a moment of peace. These folks have a unique talent for turning even the most mundane situations into high-stakes drama. They thrive on creating problems where none exist, and the drama is so contagious that you'll find yourself embroiled in conflicts you didn't even know were possible. These are the friends who turn every minor inconvenience into a five-act Shakespearean tragedy. Did they spill coffee on their shirt? That's Act I. Did someone forget to reply to their text? That's Act II. And by Act V, they're convinced the universe is conspiring against them. Your life will never lack excitement, and you'll always have a front-row seat to their never-ending performance.

To up the ante, make sure to involve yourself in their drama as much as possible. Dive headfirst into their tempestuous world. Give unsolicited advice like it's your new hobby, pick sides with all the enthusiasm of a tabloid journalist, and blow every minor issue up to epic proportions. Your life will soon be a never-ending soap opera, and you'll be the exhausted protagonist trying to keep up. Remember, the more toxic the relationship, the better the ratings.

Attract people who thrive on drama by fuelling their disputes and escalating tensions. When your friend tells you about the latest argument they had, instead of offering calming advice, respond by saying something like, *"Oh, she dared to say that? I'd have ripped her a new one!"* Watch the fireworks as your suggestion leads to an explosive confrontation. You'll never have a dull moment again.

The Emotional Vampire

If you're serious about going into depression, you need to become besties with Emotional Vampires. These people are like the Dracula of distress — forever hungry for your emotional blood. They're perpetually sad, angry, or distressed, and they love nothing more than to dump their emotional garbage on you. Want to feel perpetually drained and hopeless? Look no further. Their tactic? Endless, relentless negativity. No matter what, they'll find a way to turn a sunny day into a dark cloud of despair.

Now, don't confuse them with those charming Parasites. While they're both in the same emotional suckage family, Emotional Vampires are the top-tier professionals. They're life-suckers, while Parasites are energy-thieves. But let's not split hairs — they function quite similarly by virtue of their very existence. Both will happily drag you down to their level of despair.

These are the delightful souls who, no matter what's happening in their lives, always seem to need your undivided attention and emotional support. Expect late-night calls about the profound existential crisis triggered by their dog ignoring them. They'll expect you to drop everything and rush to their side every time they have a minor meltdown.

If you are still feeling unsatisfied with my advice or you smell any lack of conviction in it, then forget the garden-variety vampires we have been talking about; it's time for us to move on to elite Emotional Vampires. These specimens, slightly pro than their predecessors due to evolution, are so advanced that they create problems just to have something to complain about. Their never-ending cycle of self-created misery will ensure you're dragged into their vortex of despair.

The beauty of all these Emotional Vampires is that they never reciprocate. You'll pour your heart out to them, only to receive a blank stare and a quick segue back to their problems. This one-sided emotional workout is a surefire way to feel completely drained, unappreciated, and thoroughly miserable.

The Frenemy Zone

Who needs enemies when you can have frenemies? No epic tale of depression is complete without a few frenemies. These charming backstabbers smile sweetly to your face while secretly plotting your downfall. They revel in your failures and envy your successes, all while pretending to be your best buddies. It's like living in your own Game of Thrones but with more passive-aggressive comments and fewer dragons.

Imagine the thrill of having to constantly watch your back, knowing your so-called *"friends"* are always just a step away from pulling the rug out from under you. These are the friends who'll *"accidentally"* spill your secrets, undermine your achievements, and subtly sabotage your efforts. Trust me, the delightful mix of constant anxiety and suspicion that they produce for you will do wonders for your mental health. It's like living in a constant state of paranoia, wondering when they'll strike next. Keep them close — after all, what's life without a little treachery and distrust?

The Critic's Choice

Oh, just wrapped up a major project? Expect a detailed analysis of everything you did wrong. Got a new haircut? Brace yourself for a thorough deconstruction of why it's the absolute worst choice for your face shape. When it comes to self-loathing, having critics in your life is like having a never-ending buffet of self-doubt.

For the ultimate self-criticism experience, make sure your inner circle is jam-packed with these expert naysayers. Forget constructive criticism; they are for amateurs. You, my friend, need folks who specialize in destructive criticism.

These friends have a PhD in Criticism, and their favourite pastime is dissecting every aspect of your life. These are the friends who never miss an opportunity to point out your flaws, whether it's your fashion sense, career choices, or personality traits. They'll nitpick everything about you, ensuring you're always aware of your shortcomings, and will help you cultivate a healthy crop of self-doubt and insecurity.

Self-esteem? So last season. Aim for self-doubt and insecurity instead. Ensure your inner circle is filled with critics to keep you perpetually on edge. Seek their approval in everything you do. Let their negative vibes be the fuel for your self-destructive journey. Perfect for anyone looking to erode their self-confidence effectively. Who needs confidence when you can have a parade of pessimism?

The Manipulator's Club

Gaslighting isn't just for movies — it's a way of life for the Manipulator's Club. These friends are pros at making you doubt your own reality. They'll gaslight you into believing you're always wrong, even when you're clearly right. They're masters of the art of deception, using guilt, shame, and confusion to finely tune instruments to control you. They'll have you believing you're perpetually mistaken, and before you know it, you'll be questioning everything from your sanity to your shoe size. They'll twist your words, play mind games, and guilt-trip you into doing things you never wanted to do.

These friends are so skilled at getting what they want they'll make you think it was your idea all along. Their lies are so smooth that you might even start believing them yourself. Over time, you'll lose touch with your own thoughts and desires, becoming a puppet in their elaborate game. They'll contort every situation to their benefit, leaving you in a perpetual state of existential crisis. The constant mental gymnastics will keep you on edge and ensure you're always one step away from a breakdown.

The Passive-Aggressive Posse

Nothing says *"mental anguish"* quite like surrounding yourself with passive-aggressive companions. Surround yourself with these delightful individuals who make you question your sanity all the time. These friends will never confront you directly. Instead, they'll sprinkle your life with sarcastic comments, backhanded compliments, and classic silent treatments in their wake. Picture it as a twisted game show where the only prize is a lifetime supply of self-doubt.

Their specialty is saying one thing while meaning another, leaving you constantly guessing. Expect gems like *"I'm not mad, just disappointed,"* leaving you to decode the mystery of your supposed transgression. Direct confrontation? That's not their style. Instead, they'll communicate their displeasure through snide remarks and icy glares.

Imagine receiving a text that reads, *"Wow, you're actually on time for once!"* From the outside, it seems innocent enough, but it's laced with enough passive-aggressive venom to keep you doubting your punctuality all day. Treasure these moments — they're like little mental landmines. It's the perfect recipe for chronic anxiety and frustration, guaranteeing you a constant state of confusion and self-doubt.

The Martyr Syndrome

If you really want to plunge headfirst into the abyss of despair, make sure to surround yourself with friends suffering from Martyr Syndrome. These are the folks who've mastered the delicate art of victimhood, always ready with a new tale of woe, expecting you to join them in their misery. They're the eternal sufferers who have perfected the art of suffering and will ensure you know just how hard their lives are at every opportunity. They'll outdo your worst day with tales of their perpetual suffering. No matter what you're going through, they've got it worse, and they'll make sure you know it.

The magic of Martyr Syndrome lies in its infinite depth. No matter how much sympathy you offer, it's never enough. They'll continuously unearth new sources of unhappiness, dragging you down with their relentless negativity. You'll find yourself taking on their problems, feeling responsible for their perpetual state of despair. It's the perfect recipe for feeling utterly hopeless and overwhelmed. Their misery demands company, and together, you can compose a grand symphony of shared suffering.

Take Lucy, for example. She's a virtuoso in transforming any situation into a personal tragedy. Failed her exam? Clearly, the professor hates her. Her boyfriend broke up with her? He's the worst person alive. By offering her a shoulder to cry on, you get to soak up her sadness, exponentially amplifying your own. It's the ultimate win-win!

The Jealous Jamboree

What's life without a little jealousy? Welcome to the Jealous Jamboree, where the fun never ends and the compliments are non-existent! Surround yourself with friends who can't help but turn green at your every success. To ensure you never feel good about your accomplishments, stick close to those who envy every tiny triumph. These delightful folks can't bear to see you succeed. With every achievement, they'll downplay it, criticize it, or simply pretend it never happened. They'll remind you of how insignificant your successes are compared to their imagined conquests. Over time, you'll learn to downplay your own accomplishments, cultivating a beautiful sense of inadequacy.

Got a promotion? They'll remind you of their own stalled career. Found love? They'll subtly hint it won't last. It's like having your own Greek chorus of negativity, constantly reminding you that nothing you do is ever good enough. Share your successes and watch them find new and creative ways to diminish them. Their jealousy is the soundtrack to your downfall! Their envy will seep into your own mindset, making you doubt your worth and achievements.

Then there are the special few who fall into the elite group of Jealous Jamborees, who don't just envy your success but actively try to sabotage it. Their relentless efforts to drag you down to their level will ensure your achievements feel hollow and your progress perpetually stunted. Bask in the glow of their envy and watch your joy fade into oblivion!

The Competitive Frenzy

Finally, for the ultimate in self-inflicted misery, make sure to surround yourself with people who see life as a never-ending competition, ensuring you're never able to relax and you as their main rival. Every success you achieve is a threat to them, and they'll do everything they can to outshine you. Whether it's your career, relationships, social media following, or personal achievements, they'll find a way to outdo you. Got a promotion? They'll one-up you with their latest achievement. Bought a new car? They'll boast about their superior model. The constant comparison will keep you on edge, fostering a lovely sense of perpetual dissatisfaction. Their relentless drive to outdo you will keep you in a state of constant stress and insecurity, perfectly aligned with your goal of spiralling into depression.

This daily dose of cutthroat rivalry will keep you on edge, constantly striving to prove yourself while feeling inadequate. It's the perfect way to erode your self-confidence and fuel your insecurities. Enjoy the thrill of the chase and watch your stress levels soar to new heights.

Practical Exercises

To help you master these techniques, here are some practical exercises:

1. ***Plan a Drama-Filled Event:*** Organize a get-together with your most dramatic friends. Ensure there's plenty of alcohol and controversial topics to discuss. Watch the chaos unfold, and make sure to insert yourself into every conflict.

2. ***Host a Critique Session:*** Invite your critic friends over for a *"constructive feedback"* session. Present them with your latest achievements and ask for their honest opinions. Take notes on their harshest criticisms and reflect on them daily.

3. ***Join a Passive-Aggressive Group Chat:*** Start or join a group chat with passive-aggressive friends. Pay close attention to their sarcastic comments and backhanded compliments. Try to respond in a way that's equally passive-aggressive, and keep track of your growing frustration.

4. ***Offer Unlimited Emotional Support:*** Make yourself available 24/7 to your Emotional Vampire friends. Answer their late-night calls, drop everything to comfort them, and avoid seeking any support in return. Notice how drained and unappreciated you feel afterward.

5. ***Engage in Friendly Competition:*** Challenge your competitive friends to various activities, from sports to

career achievements. Observe how their rivalry affects your self-esteem and sense of accomplishment.

6. ***Reflect on Your Frenemy's Actions:*** Keep a journal of your interactions with frenemies. Write down instances of betrayal, sabotage, and undermining. Reflect on how these actions make you feel and how they contribute to your overall sense of mistrust and paranoia.

7. ***Immerse in Martyr Tales:*** Spend time listening to your Martyr friends' endless tales of woe. Offer sympathy and support, but don't expect any positivity in return. Reflect on how their constant negativity affects your own mood.

8. ***Practice Being Manipulated:*** Allow your manipulative friends to dictate your actions and decisions. Notice the confusion and self-doubt that arise from their gaslighting and mind games.

9. ***Enjoy the Jealous Vibes:*** Share your successes with jealous friends and observe their reactions. Take note of their envy and how it makes you question the validity of your achievements.

Congratulations! If you've diligently followed our foolproof guide to surround yourself with toxic people, you're well on your way to mastering the fine art of personal misery. By now, you should be a seasoned connoisseur of attracting energy vampires, drama magnets, and emotional leeches. Your social circle, now a delightful cesspool of negativity, is tailor-made to ensure that every waking moment is a masterclass in self-degradation. Happiness? Who needs it? With this elite squad of joy-suckers, you'll revel in unparalleled levels of despair and self-doubt. So, raise a glass to your new toxic entourage — here's to endless drama, relentless criticism, and a life so tumultuous it makes reality TV look like a breezy vacation.

***

Chapter 3

"Work-Life Imbalance"

Welcome to Chapter 3 of *"An Epic Guide to Go into Depression."* If you're tired of trivial pursuits like happiness, relaxation, and general well-being, you've come to the right place. This chapter is your golden ticket to a life where work is your sole companion and balance is just a fairy tale for the uninitiated.

But fear not! This isn't just about highlighting the woes of the overworked. We're here to equip you with practical exercises to ensure you, too, can master the art of extreme depression. We're diving headfirst into the blissful void of work-life imbalance, where the only thing more stretched than your sanity is your overbooked calendar. Get ready to revel in the grind — because who needs a personal life when you can bask in the glow of professional success? So, adjust your ties, buff up those resumes, and let's plunge into the exhilarating, soul-crushing, and oddly irresistible realm of work-life imbalance. Your quest to perfect depression begins now!

The Workaholic's Anthem

Your mornings commence at the ungodly hour when most sane people are still dreaming of their bed. Coffee in hand, you arrive at the office before the sun has even considered rising. The janitors greet you with reverent nods, acknowledging your role as the office's very own productivity prophet. Your workday is a relentless parade of emails, meetings, and tasks, tackled with the enthusiasm of a zealot on a caffeine high. To you, work isn't just a job; it's your entire personality.

It's 2 AM, and while the mere mortals are indulging in dreams of sandy beaches and fruity cocktails, you're engrossed in crafting a PowerPoint presentation that will probably be glanced at once and promptly forgotten. Nothing quite compares to the joy of making your job your sole identity. Forget hobbies, friendships, or any semblance of a personal life. Inspirational posters adorn the walls, each screaming slogans like *"Grind Until You Shine"* and *"Success Never Sleeps."* Your desk is a shrine to productivity, cluttered with motivational books you've never read because you're too busy working.

Your weekends? A distant memory. They're now just extra days to get ahead on next week's workload. Who needs them when you can bask in the fluorescent glory of office lights? *"Sleep? Pfft, that's for mortals!"* you chant as you sip your fifth cup of coffee. Sleep is overrated, anyway. Your life is an unending verse of spreadsheets and deadlines, with the chorus proudly proclaiming, *"I can sleep when I'm dead!"*

Ah, what a harmonious life if by harmony you mean the sound of your sanity quietly sobbing in the background. What matters is that you respond to that 2 AM email within five minutes, proving your dedication to the cause. After all, nothing screams commitment like being perpetually exhausted and slightly delirious.

Forget the trivial matters of family dinners and leisure time. They are but distractions from the holy grail of productivity. Your family has learned not to expect you at gatherings; they know you're chasing something greater than simple companionship — you're chasing the elusive dream of being irreplaceable. Every missed birthday, and every ignored phone call from your loved ones is just another testament to your undying commitment to the corporate cause.

The Burnout Express

Experience the exquisite joy of running on empty while maintaining the illusion of competence. Remember, nothing says dedication like collapsing at your desk. Those dark circles under your eyes aren't distress signals; they are badges of honour. Wear them proudly, like a war hero fresh from the front lines of the corporate battlefield.

Your day starts before it even begins. Tossing and turning in bed, you mentally run through the tasks awaiting you. As the sun peeks over the horizon, you're already buried in emails, setting the pace for a day that never seems to end.

This isn't just about putting in extra hours — no, no, no. This is about living and breathing your job. Forget about eating healthy or taking breaks. Your body might despise you, but hey, at least your email response time is impeccable! And isn't that what really matters? Remember, it's not about the destination; it's about the journey — specifically, the journey to a nervous breakdown.

Your lunch break? An opportunity to multitask. Why waste precious time eating when you can perfect that PowerPoint presentation? Food becomes an afterthought, a mere pit stop on your race to the finish line. You work tirelessly, fuelled by caffeine and sheer willpower. Colleagues wonder if you're a cyborg, capable of operating without the need for rest. *"You're a machine!"* they say, and you beam with pride.

Evenings morph into nights, with only your desk lamp providing any semblance of light in the otherwise deserted office. Your phone never stops pinging, and you respond with the urgency of a superhero, no matter the hour. Your body might scream for rest, but you'll silence it with another shot of espresso. Sleep is for the faint-hearted, and you, my friend, are anything but.

Feel the adrenaline rush as deadlines loom and stress hits the roof. Admire your ability to function on four hours of sleep and a diet of vending machine leftovers. Your immune system might throw a tantrum, but who cares about minor inconveniences like health? You're too busy riding the rails of relentless ambition, speeding past the signs warning you of impending burnout.

As the weeks turn into months, your body starts to protest. Fatigue sets in, but you push through it, driven by the fear of falling behind. Your work becomes a marathon with no finish line, and you're determined to stay ahead, no matter the cost.

But wait, there's more! The Burnout Express offers complimentary stress, anxiety, and a delightful sprinkle of existential dread. You'll be the envy of your colleagues with your impressive productivity and the subtle twitch in your eye that indicates you haven't slept properly in weeks. Who needs rest when you can be a corporate hero, valiantly fighting off the urge to collapse from sheer exhaustion?

The Meeting Marathon

If there's one thing more exhilarating than the grind, it's the thrill of the Meeting Marathon, a sensational event where your calendar transforms into a chaotic Tetris game from hell. The objective? To schedule back-to-back meetings until you can't remember what daylight looks like. Bonus points if you can fit in a few more meetings during your bathroom breaks! Experience the thrill of leaping from one Zoom call to the next with no time to actually absorb any information or even sip a glass of water. You're a meeting machine, an unstoppable force of corporate efficiency. The goal here is to ensure you have no time to actually do any work.

After all, the more meetings you have, the more important you appear.

Marvel at the ingenuity of creating meetings to plan other meetings. Revel in the joy of endless video calls where everyone talks, but nothing gets done. Feel the rush of adrenaline as you juggle multiple time zones and agendas, all while trying to remember what the meeting was actually about. If you're truly fortunate, you might even get to experience the thrill of double-booking yourself to attend two meetings at once. Dual screens are not just for gamers! Your colleagues will admire your ability to be omnipresent, and you'll take pride in your multitasking genius.

Forget about actually doing tasks; discussing them in excruciating detail is where the real excitement lies. Your reward? The satisfaction of knowing you've spent your day in the most inefficient way possible. Forget the content of these meetings. What matters is the quantity. Your days will blur into a never-ending series of Zoom calls, where you master the art of pretending to listen while secretly checking your emails.

Forget bathroom breaks or lunch; those are luxuries for the unambitious. Imagine you're in your seventh hour of consecutive meetings, your bladder is on the verge of rebellion right to the brink of a probable leakage, threatening everyone around you with an unwanted splash, and your stomach has forgotten what food is. Each meeting bleeds into the next, and by the end of the day, you have no idea what was discussed, who attended, or what language anyone was speaking. But hey, you attended every single one of them! Take pride in that.

By the end of the week, you'll have perfected the blank stare and nod combo, signalling both engagement and utter detachment. Your family might forget what you look like, but at least your colleagues will know you're always available for a quick chat about quarterly projections. Who needs productivity when you can dedicate your entire day to discussing productivity in endless meetings?

The Task Juggler

Ever dreamt of joining a circus? Well, now's your chance! Embrace the role of the Task Juggler, balancing so many tasks at once that you could put professional performers to shame. Emails, reports, presentations, and projects — all tossed into the air with the grace of a circus performer. The secret is to keep adding more balls until the inevitable disaster strikes. Why be good at one thing when you can be mediocre at many?

Task juggling is an art form. Imagine your day begins with a flurry of activity. Emails pouring in from all corners, each one demanding immediate attention. Phone calls interrupt your train of thought, but you handle them with the grace of a seasoned performer. Meetings are squeezed in between the tasks, leaving you no time to catch your breath. Your brain is in overdrive, your stress levels are through the roof, and your productivity has taken a nosedive. You pride yourself on your ability to multitask. One moment, you're drafting a report; the next, you're on a conference call, all while responding to instant messages. Your colleagues marvel at your efficiency, unaware of the chaos brewing beneath the surface.

Feel the thrill as you attempt to balance urgent deadlines with mundane tasks. Juggle those tasks like a pro, and watch as your to-do list becomes a source of anxiety and dread. Your to-do list grows longer by the minute, and your desk resembles a war zone of sticky notes and half-finished reports. But who cares about quality when you can achieve sheer quantity? The secret to this act is to never, ever delegate. Every task is your responsibility, and you alone must bear the burden.

The thrill of task juggling lies in its unpredictability. Take on every project that comes your way, no matter how trivial or overwhelming. After all, saying no is for those who lack ambition, and you are not one of them. Each day presents a new set of challenges, and you rise to meet them with unflagging determination. Deadlines loom, but you tackle them head-on, refusing to let anything slip through the cracks.

But as the days turn into weeks, the strain begins to show. Tasks pile up faster than you can handle them, and you struggle to keep everything in balance. Watch in awe as you balance a million tasks at once, each one more critical than the last. The once exhilarating challenge now feels like a burden, with each new task adding weight to your load.

As you juggle, you'll experience the thrill of teetering on the edge of chaos, the adrenaline rush of knowing that at any moment, everything could come crashing down. And crash it will, in a magnificent display of missed deadlines and half-finished work. Things are bound to drop, and when they do, it's everyone else's fault but yours. But hey, at least you tried, right? That's got to count for something. The spectacle is in the attempt, not the result.

The Email Obsession

Let's not forget the Email Obsession, a delightful exercise in digital madness. Your day revolves around your inbox. Your mission, should you choose to accept it, is to check your emails every five minutes, even during meetings. Yes, even at 2 AM. After all, who needs sleep when there are unread messages in your inbox? Ignore the toll on your mental health; the real tragedy would be missing an email. Sleep is for the weak, and you are anything but not weak, at least!

Sleep becomes a distant memory as you wake up at odd hours to check your emails. You pride yourself on your quick response time, often replying within minutes of receiving a message. Your colleagues wonder how you manage to stay so connected, and you smile, knowing that your secret is simple: relentless dedication.

But as the days pass, the constant barrage of emails begins to take its toll. You feel a growing sense of anxiety, knowing that each new message demands your attention.

The thrill of staying connected fades, replaced by a sense of dread as your inbox fills faster than you can empty it.

Email addiction is the gateway to constant stress. Your phone becomes an extension of your hand vibrating with every new notification, always ready to alert you to the latest email from Marketing about the new company mascot. The dopamine hit from each new message keeps you going, fuelling your insomnia with the sweet nectar of corporate communication. You respond instantly, no matter the time or place, determined to maintain your reputation for promptness. And you wouldn't want anyone thinking you have a life outside of work, now, would you?

That's the life of an email obsessive. Your dreams are just as stressful as your waking hours. Your family might miss you, but hey, those emails aren't going to read themselves. The goal is to never let your inbox reach zero because a perpetually full inbox is a sign of your importance. Remember, sleep is overrated when there's always another email waiting, and when you're awake at all hours, you're not just losing sleep; you're losing your mind.

The Office Nomad

For the true work-life imbalance specialist, we present The Office Nomad. Transform your office into your second home, complete with a sleeping bag under your desk and a toothbrush in your drawer. Your desk is a fortress of productivity, perfect with all the comforts of home. You spend so much time there that the cleaning crew knows you by name. You've even decorated your desk with family photos, making it a truly homey environment. Who says home is where the heart is? For you, home is where the Wi-Fi is strongest.

Spend your nights under the comforting hum of the air conditioner and the gentle glow of your computer screen. Who needs a cozy bed or quality time with loved ones when you have deadlines to meet and PowerPoints to perfect? You might forget the way to your actual home, but rest assured, you'll be the most dedicated employee in the building.

The office is where you spend most of your waking hours. You've staked out your territory, claiming a corner where you can work undisturbed. Your colleagues marvel at your dedication, often finding you at your desk long after they've gone home. They might even whisper behind your back, but little do they know the joy of never truly leaving work. Shower in the office gym, dine on vending machine delicacies and make your cubicle as cozy as possible. After all, why would you ever want to leave?

Lunch breaks are spent at your desk, catching up on emails and finishing tasks. You rarely leave the office, preferring the convenience of your workspace. Your phone is always within reach, and you're never more than a few steps away from your computer.

But again, as the days turn into weeks and weeks into months, the isolation begins to weigh on you. The office, once a place of productivity, now feels like a prison.

You miss the simple pleasures of home, the comfort of a bed, and the warmth of family. The convenience of the office fades, replaced by a longing for a life beyond work.

But you want to experience the joy of having no boundaries between work and home. Your coworkers become your surrogate family, and the office fridge is your pantry. Feel the pride as you watch the cleaning crew come and go while you remain steadfast at your desk. The goal is to blur the lines so thoroughly that you forget where work ends and life begins.

The No Vacation Policy

Ah, vacations. A time for rest, relaxation, and… wait, what are those again? That's just a foreign concept for those who don't have their priorities straight. You'll never know because you've mastered The No Vacation Policy. Accumulate so much vacation time that you could take a year off but never actually use it. The thrill of knowing you have days off but never taking them is a special kind of torture. Vacations are for quitters, and you, my friend, are no quitter.

Watch as your colleagues post envy-inducing pictures on Instagram from their 3000-miles-long road trip while you remain steadfast at your desk, churning out reports and attending meetings. You wear your unused vacation days like a badge of honour, a testament to your unwavering commitment to the grind. Who needs a break when you can have a breakdown instead?

Your calendar is a testament to your dedication. Weeks and months pass without a single day off. You pride yourself on your work ethic, convinced that taking time off is a sign of weakness. Your colleagues envy your unused vacation days, unaware of the toll it takes on you. But as the months turn into years, the strain begins to show. You long for a break, a chance to recharge and escape the grind. But it is the crown jewel of work-life imbalance!

Feel the satisfaction of knowing your vacation days are piling up like an untouched treasure trove. Ignore the envy of your colleagues as they jet off to exotic locations while you remain firmly planted at your desk. The sun, sand, and relaxation are but distractions from your true purpose. Every unused vacation day is a testament to your commitment, a reminder that you are indispensable. The goal is to retire with a mountain of unused vacation days, a true testament to your work ethic.

The Family Stranger

In the grand tradition of sacrificing everything for your job, we introduce The Family Stranger. Ensure your family only sees you in passing, like a friendly ghost who occasionally haunts the house. You might live under the same roof, but your presence is as fleeting as a mirage. Your presence at home is so rare that your family starts to forget what you look like. When your child asks who you are, you know you've reached peak work-life imbalance. When you do appear, it's a momentous occasion filled with awkward small talk and questions about your mysterious work life. After all, family time is overrated when there are reports to be filed and emails to be answered.

Family dinners? Those are for people with balanced lives. Weekend outings? Not in this lifetime. Your kids' school plays, your partner's birthday bash, family movie nights — all distant memories as you prioritize late nights at the office over quality time at home. Pop in for dinner just long enough to remind them what you look like. Your family might start leaving sticky notes on the fridge to remind you of their names, but that's a small price to pay for being the MVP (most valuable person) of your workplace.

Your family learns to carry on without you. Weekends are spent catching up on work, leaving little time for them. You tell yourself that you're doing it for them and that your hard work will pay off in the end. But as the weeks turn into months, the distance between you and your family grows.

The thrill of being a dedicated worker fades as you realize what you've sacrificed. Your family, once a source of joy, now feels like strangers. You long for a chance to reconnect, but the demands of work keep pulling you away. But don't worry; the workplace will always be there to fill the void of familial connections.

Feel the pang of guilt as you miss yet another family event, but quickly brush it aside. The office needs you more than your children do, right? Your spouse might yearn for your company, but those emails won't answer themselves.

The goal is to create a life where your family becomes accustomed to your absence, relying on photos and fond memories to remember what you look like. The ultimate achievement? Becoming a legend in your own home, talked about but rarely seen. After all, providing for them financially is more important than actually spending time with them, right?

The Achievement Addict

Next, we have The Achievement Addict. Nothing says success, like chasing achievements and accolades, until you're a hollow shell of your former self. Trophies make great headstones, and you're determined to collect them all.

Every promotion, every award, every pat on the back fuels your addiction, pushing you further down the path of workaholism. You might forget what genuine joy feels like, but who needs that when you have the fleeting satisfaction of another accolade? Your life becomes a series of checkboxes, each one ticked off with the precision of a surgeon, leaving little room for anything — or anyone — else.

Sacrifice your well-being in the pursuit of recognition. Every award you receive brings a momentary high, quickly replaced by the need for another. Your self-worth becomes tied to external validation, and you chase it relentlessly, ignoring the toll it takes on your mental health and happiness. Your life is a never-ending quest for recognition.

The thrill of achievement drives you forward, pushing you to take on more and more. You sign up for courses, pursue certifications, and tackle new challenges with unflagging determination. But as time flies by, the pursuit of achievement begins to feel hollow.

Feel the rush of adrenaline as you climb the corporate ladder, each rung marked by another accolade. Your office wall becomes a shrine to your success, adorned with certificates and plaques. The satisfaction of another achievement quickly fades, replaced by the relentless pursuit of the next one. Ignore the toll it takes on your physical health and relationships; they are but minor sacrifices in the grand scheme of things. The goal is to accumulate so many achievements that they overshadow your very existence, leaving a legacy of hollow victories.

The Martyr at Work

No chapter on work-life imbalance is complete without The Martyr at Work. Burnout is just a sign of dedication, right? You sacrifice your time, energy, and well-being to show that you are indispensable. Every project, every task, every new responsibility is a chance to prove your mettle.

Watch as your colleagues are amazed at your willingness to shoulder every burden, tackle every task, and solve every problem. They might even start calling you *"the office hero,"* but deep down, you know the truth. You're not a hero; you're a martyr, sacrificing your well-being on the altar of corporate success. And when you inevitably burn out, at least you'll have the satisfaction of knowing you gave it your all.

You volunteer for every task, take on every project, and never say no. Feel the weight of the world on your shoulders as you juggle multiple projects with ease. The thrill of being indispensable is worth the exhaustion and stress. Ignore the warning signs of burnout, for they are but minor obstacles on your path to greatness. The goal is to become the ultimate martyr, sacrificing your well-being for the sake of your work.

The more you suffer, the more valuable you feel. Ignore the voice in your head begging for rest; true commitment means sacrificing everything for the job. Your colleagues might admire your dedication, but they'll also steer clear, knowing that your path is one of inevitable self-destruction. But who needs friends or social life when you have the sweet, bitter taste of professional martyrdom?

Practical Exercises

To help you master these techniques and truly embrace the joys of work-life imbalance, here are some practical exercises:

1. ***Workaholic Warm-Up:*** Start your day with a motivational email to yourself at 5 AM.

2. ***Burnout Blitz:*** Skip lunch breaks for a week and see how many extra tasks you can complete.

3. ***Meeting Madness:*** Schedule a meeting to discuss why you have too many meetings.

4. ***Task Juggling****:* Attempt to complete three major projects simultaneously without any help.

5. ***Email Alert****:* Set your email notifications to go off every minute. Respond immediately.

6. ***Nomadic Nights****:* Spend one night a week sleeping at the office.

7. ***Vacation Veto****:* Plan a vacation but cancel it at the last minute due to work commitments.

8. ***Family Fade****:* Walk past your family during dinner, wave, and head back to your home office.

9. ***Achievement Chase****:* Sign up for an online course every month and never finish any of them.

10. ***Martyr Marathon****:* Volunteer for an extra project every time someone else declines.

And there you have it, Folks — the grand tour of the grindhouse is complete. Hearty congratulations on making it through this chapter. You're now equipped with the tools to turn your life into a finely tuned instrument of professional misery. By incorporating these exercises into your daily routine, you'll be well on your way to achieving the ultimate work-life imbalance. Your inbox will never be empty, your calendar will never have a free slot, and your family will always wonder who that mysterious person in their home office is.

As you step off this rollercoaster of relentless productivity and onto the platform of perpetual exhaustion, remember that the key to mastering work-life imbalance is commitment. Commit to ignoring your health, your family, and your happiness. Embrace the chaos and let it consume you until you're at a lips distance away from peak depression. Happy grinding!

***

"The Art of Self-Criticism"

Welcome, dear reader, to Chapter 4 of our epic journey into the depths of despair, *"The Art of Self-Criticism."* If you're looking to plunge yourself headfirst into the abyss of depression, look no further! You have landed yourself in the right place.

Self-criticism is an essential tool in your melancholic arsenal. We will explore the most effective ways to make yourself your own worst enemy and critique yourself with the precision and intensity of a professional heckler. So, grab a mirror and a magnifying glass, and let's dive into the devastating world of self-criticism.

The Mirror's Worst Enemy

Mornings are a time of hope and renewal for many, but not for you, my friend. As soon as you wake up, drag yourself to your nearest mirror and begin the ritual. This is no ordinary mirror; this is the gateway to your soul's deepest insecurities. Start every day by pointing out every flaw you see in the mirror. Not just the obvious ones — no, that would be too easy. See that tiny blemish on your cheek? Disastrous! That single grey hair? Catastrophic! Be relentless.

If you're still feeling particularly adventurous, invest in a magnifying glass of fine quality, the largest you can afford. Now, start with the glaring imperfections: that zit that popped up overnight, the dark circles under your eyes or how that one tooth is slightly crooked, and the asymmetrical eyebrows. Move on to more subtle imperfections: the tiny wrinkle that no one but you can see, the slight unevenness in your skin tone, and the barely noticeable frizz in your hair. Think of it as your own personal game of *"Spot the Difference,"* except you're the only player, and the difference is always that you looked better yesterday. What a delightful way to set the tone for the day! Remember, no flaw is too small to obsess over.

The goal is to feel progressively worse about yourself the longer you stare. This ritual should be done with the intensity of a detective at a crime scene, where the crime is the mere existence of your reflection. With enough dedication, you can turn this daily habit into an Olympic-level event just for yourself. You'll become an expert at finding issues where there were none before, a true artist of self-doubt and misery. Your aim is to ensure you leave that mirror with your self-esteem lower than your basement and continue your journey into the abyss of depression.

The Internal Critic

Meet your new best friend: your inner voice, but not the kind that gives you pep talks. No, this one's got the intensity of a drill sergeant without encouragement. It should accompany you throughout the day, making sure you never forget how spectacularly awful you are at everything. It should be there to remind you that you're not just bad at something; you're epically terrible. Couldn't even pour a cup of coffee without spilling it? Pathetic! Messed up a presentation? Clearly, you're an embarrassment to humanity! Self-love? Pfft. That's for amateurs who haven't mastered the fine art of self-loathing.

Every time you consider giving yourself a break, remind yourself that a true critic never rests. If your inner monologue doesn't make you want to crawl under a rock, you're not doing it right. True mastery lies in cultivating an unyielding self-criticism that leaves no room for any semblance of self-esteem. The key here is consistency — never let a positive thought sneak in. Remember, the more brutal and unforgiving you are, the closer you get to achieving the ultimate goal: a deeply ingrained sense of worthlessness and depression.

The Negative Nelly

Ah, compliments. Those rare, fleeting moments when someone says something nice about you. How to handle them? Simple: crush them with a self-deprecating remark. Compliments are like boomerangs — they should come back to haunt you. So, the next time someone gives you a compliment, make sure to counter it with a self-deprecating remark. When one person says, *"You look nice today,"* respond with, *"Oh, I must be doing something wrong then."* If someone else says, *"You look nice today,"* respond with, *"Oh, you must be blind."* Does someone praise your work? *"It's not that great, I just got lucky."* This is the kind of exchange that keeps conversations lively and people perplexed.

Responding to praise with a self-deprecating remark isn't just a tactic; it's another form of art. It's a great way to kill conversations and reinforce your commitment to self-criticism. Perfect it, and you'll be the life of the party — the party everyone avoids inviting you to because you're such a buzzkill.

This technique is excellent for always killing conversations and ensuring people eventually stop trying to compliment you and think twice before being nice to you again. Extra credits to you if you can make the compliment-giver slightly uncomfortable. Always be ready with a downbeat response to any positive comment.

The Comparison Game

Why just feel bad about yourself in isolation when you can compare yourself to others and feel even worse? Social media is your perfect partner in this endeavour! Scroll through Instagram, LinkedIn, Facebook, and every other platform to see just how much more successful, attractive, and happy everyone else is. And guess what? Everyone is!

Playing the Comparison Game is the ultimate way to make sure you never feel good enough. Imagine running a marathon with no finish line, except you're running backward, and everyone else is cruising ahead on bikes. Don't forget that everyone is better than you, and that's a fact you need to reaffirm constantly.

Spend a delightful hour scrolling through your social feeds and focus on the lives that seem perfect as compared to your series of unfortunate events. Identify colleagues who are better at their jobs. Your co-worker got a promotion? Your friend bought a house? Perfect — fuel for your ever-burning self-doubt fire.

Don't forget to take notes on the life choices of your siblings, friends, and even that guy you met once at a party. They all seem so much happier and fulfilled. Keep this up, and you'll be spiralling into despair in no time. Remember, their lives are undoubtedly better than yours in every conceivable way. Your job is to perpetually remind yourself of this irrefutable fact until your self-esteem is nothing but a distant memory.

The Perfectionist's Curse

Setting high standards is for amateurs. Set impossibly high standards and watch yourself crumble spectacularly. Aim for the stars, miss by a mile, and crash into a pit of despair. The beauty of this approach is that it guarantees failure. For example, aim to complete a year's worth of work in a week, achieve flawless physical fitness overnight, and master a new language by tomorrow. When you fall short (which you inevitably will), you can berate yourself for being the failure you always knew you were. The key is to turn every minor setback into a monumental disaster. This foolproof strategy ensures you never experience a moment of satisfaction.

Aim for the galaxies, miss spectacularly, and dive headfirst into a black hole of self-disappointment. Whether it's work, relationships, or hobbies, your mission is to set such sky-high standards that you can bask in the warm glow of perpetual dissatisfaction. Perfection is an elusive beast, but chasing it is a surefire way to feel inadequate. After all, success isn't about achieving goals; it's about punishing yourself for not being perfect.

The Regretful Reminiscence

Ah, the past — a treasure trove of regrets and cringe-worthy moments. Who needs happy memories when you can obsess over your greatest hits of shame and regret? Dwell on that embarrassing moment from high school as if it happened yesterday. Relive every awkward conversation, every questionable decision, every failed attempt, every cringe-worthy moment you've ever experienced. Hold them close, cherish them, and replay them in your mind every night before bed. Sweet dreams are overrated when you can toss and turn into a sea of regrets.

Spend your free time replaying these memories in vivid detail. Recall that charming incident when you tripped in front of your crush? Or when you said something awkward in a meeting? Relive these moments with the intensity of a cinematic masterpiece. Share these blunders with everyone you meet; nothing like a good old self-deprecating tale to keep your past failures fresh and entertaining. These aren't just any memories; they're the ones that make you cringe so hard you wish the ground would swallow you whole. Cherish them like rare collectibles. The goal is to let these memories marinate until they form a rich, regret-flavoured stew of self-loathing. This technique is all about turning your mind into a museum of personal failures. Why focus on the present when the past offers so many opportunities for self-flagellation? The more embarrassing, the better. If you're not turning red with shame at least once a day, you're not reminiscing hard enough. After all, what better way to ensure you never move forward?

The Fault Finder

Everyone makes mistakes, but you're special. You don't just make mistakes; you obsess over them. Become a forensic expert of your own failures. Identify every tiny error and magnify it until it becomes a colossal failure in your mind. It's like being your own worst enemy but with better accuracy. Made a typo in an email? Clearly, you're unfit for any professional responsibility. Accidentally used the wrong word in a conversation? Time to question your entire education. The goal here is to make every tiny mistake feel like the end of the world.

Perfection is unattainable, so focus on every tiny mistake you make. As soon as you stumble, halt all progress and give that error the attention it absolutely doesn't deserve. Ignore any context or mitigating factors. Keep a detailed record of every mistake. Make sure others are aware of your mistakes. It's not enough to feel bad internally; external acknowledgment is key. Regularly review your errors to ensure they remain at the forefront of your mind. The more you unearth, the more you'll master this delightful art of self-sabotage. With enough practice, you'll master the art of turning every tiny mistake into a personal disaster.

The Apology Machine

Apologize for everything. Bump into a chair? Apologize profusely. Someone else steps on your foot? Apologize for having feet in their way. The sun didn't shine today? Apologize. Apologize for the weather, for existing, for things entirely out of your control. This isn't just about being polite; it's about ingraining in yourself a deep-seated sense of unworthiness. Make grovelling your morning mantra and watch your self-esteem plummet beautifully.

Go on and perfect the art of unnecessary apologizing. Make sure to apologize for existing whenever possible. This delightful exercise is all about claiming unnecessary guilt as your own. The more you apologize, the more you'll convince yourself that every little mishap in the universe is somehow your responsibility. Not only will you bolster your sense of inadequacy, but you'll also cement your reputation as the perpetually sorry individual. Cheers to lowering your self-esteem with style!

The Pessimistic Prophet

Optimism is for fools. Why waste time with positive thinking when you can revel in the delightful anticipation of catastrophe? Prepare for the worst in every situation, and you'll never be disappointed. Expect failure at every turn, and predict disappointment in every endeavour. If something can go wrong, it will, and it's your job to foresee it all. The key is to maintain a bleak outlook on life, always preparing for the worst-case scenario. This way, you can live in a constant state of anxiety and dread, which is fantastic for cultivating a depressive mindset. Why bother with hope when you can luxuriate in despair?

Predict failure in everything you do. This technique is all about setting yourself up for failure before you even begin. When things inevitably crumble, you can bask in the satisfaction of having been right all along. When you start a new project, immediately think of all the ways it could go wrong. And if, by some cosmic joke, things actually succeed, you can always chalk it up to an inexplicable fluke.

Realism is the key, but not the kind that acknowledges potential success — only the kind that anticipates failure. By always expecting the worst, you'll never be disappointed — only perpetually miserable. It's a plan so foolproof it practically guarantees a lifetime of misery.

The Success Saboteur

For you, success is just a failure in disguise. Did you achieve something? Undermine your own achievements by focusing on what could have been better. Got a promotion? Remember all the mistakes you made along the way. Finished a project? Pick apart every flaw. Success isn't to be celebrated; it's to be scrutinized and dissected until you find something to be disappointed about. Every triumph is just another golden opportunity to remind yourself of how utterly inadequate you are.

Embrace the thrill of never letting success feel like anything more than an excuse for more self-deprecating analysis!

Practical Exercises

To help you master these techniques, here are some practical exercises:

1. ***Morning Mirror Madness:*** Spend five minutes each morning listing every flaw you see.

2. ***Internal Critic Drill:*** Write down the harshest critique you can think of for every task you complete.

3. ***Compliment Crusher:*** Practice turning compliments into self-deprecating remarks.

4. ***Comparison Countdown:*** List ten people more successful than you and dwell on why you'll never measure up.

5. ***Perfectionist Punishment:*** Set a goal, fail, and write an essay on why you're a failure.

6. ***Regret Rewind:*** Replay a past mistake in your head for ten minutes before bed.

7. ***Fault Finder's Diary:*** Keep a diary of every tiny mistake you make each day.

8. ***Apology Avalanche:*** Apologize for five things that aren't your fault daily.

9. ***Pessimistic Prediction:*** Predict failure in three upcoming events and explain why.

10. ***Success Sabotage:*** For every achievement, write down five things you could have done better.

Congratulations, you've just unlocked the ultimate guide to perfecting the art of self-criticism! With these handy tools, you're primed to bask in a glorious state of perpetual self-doubt and unhappiness.

Remember, achieving peak depression isn't a quick fix; it's a long, gruelling marathon of misery. So, revel in your inner critic, hold onto those regrets like cherished trophies, and fine-tune the craft of pessimism. Who needs joy when you can have the warm, comforting embrace of endless self-doubt and anxiety?

Here's to a life brimming with more self-criticism than happiness, more regret than pride, and more apologies than victories. Cheers to your endless quest to be your own harshest critic! Happy self-deprecation! You're absolutely nailing it — because, of course, that's the entire point.

***

"Exercise: How to Avoid It"

Welcome, dear reader, to Chapter 5 of *"An Epic Guide to Go into Depression,"* where we delve into the fine art of transforming your natural inclination towards inactivity into a finely honed skill set. While the world is busy glorifying sweat and muscle aches, we're here to present you with the ultimate antidote to this madness.

Why chase endorphins when you can embrace the sweet, sweet comfort of inactivity? If you've ever looked at a treadmill and felt a deep sense of existential dread, you're in precisely the right place. Here, we'll dig into the Couch Potato Creed, the fears of the Gym-phobe, and other delightfully sedentary lifestyles that will ensure your body remains in a permanent state of lethargy.

So, put on your comfiest pyjamas, grab a bag of chips, and let's embark on this journey to becoming the best couch potato you can be. Remember, the goal here is to embrace inactivity with open arms — or at least with arms that barely move.

The Couch Potato Creed

Let's start with the cornerstone of our philosophy: the Couch Potato Creed. The couch is not just a piece of furniture; it's a way of life; it's your sanctuary, your fortress of slothitude. Imagine your sofa as the most understanding, non-judgmental friend you've ever had. It doesn't care if you're binge-watching *"Stranger Things"* for the third time or if you haven't showered in days. In fact, it encourages it.

Perfecting the art of couch lounging is no small feat. It's not about just sitting down; it's about mastering the delicate balance of not moving. Seek out that elusive sweet spot where you can reach your snacks, your beer, the remote, and maybe even your phone charger without moving. Everything should be within arm's reach or at least a leg's distance away. This trifecta of laziness ensures that you remain seated for hours, possibly days, and in winter, even hibernate. In case of emergency, have an insect net tied to the end of an extendable selfie stick to grab whatever is urgent and important — everything except work. If you feel any urge to rise, remember: the more you sit, the less you move and fewer chances you have of injuring yourself by, well, moving.

The Gym-phobe

Next, let's cultivate a phobia of gyms so strong it rivals arachnophobia. Gyms are terrifying places filled with sweaty strangers, complicated machinery, and mirrors that cruelly reflect your every move. To solidify your gym-phobia, start by visualizing all the horrors that await you there. Picture yourself tripping on the treadmill, dropping a dumbbell on your foot, or, worse yet, being approached by a perky trainer offering unsolicited advice.

Instead, proudly flaunt your fear. Develop a comprehensive list of excuses to avoid gyms at all costs. Common ones include:

- *"I can't go today; I just washed my hair."*

- *"I heard someone got ringworm from the locker room."*

- *"I don't want to get too muscular."*

- *"I can't go to the gym; it's flu season, and I heard weights are a breeding ground for germs."*

With these excuses, you'll never have to set foot in a gym again. After all, who needs weights when you have excuses?

The Elevator Enthusiast

Another key strategy is to become an Elevator Enthusiast. The stairs? Please note that those are for peasants and marathon runners. You are way about their league. Elevators are where it's at. Make a commitment to yourself, like a New Year resolution on the very first day of the year, to always take the elevator, even if it's just one floor in either direction. This dedication to vertical transportation will ensure you never accidentally burn a calorie.

To fully immerse yourself in this lifestyle, consider downloading an elevator finder app if available at your geographical region. This way, you'll never have to face the horror of a staircase again. If an elevator is out of order, don't hesitate to wait. Stand there confidently with a smug grin, wait for an engineer to come and fix it for you, even if it takes hours, days, weeks or even months. After all, you're preserving your invaluable energy with such heroic patience.

The Remote Reach

Perfecting the art of the Remote Reach without moving from your spot is essential. This technique is a high-level skill in maintaining supreme comfort while reaching for the TV remote, chips, or refreshing beverage without so much as shifting your glorious lounging position. It's a form of yoga, but without the effort or annoying mindfulness.

Start with small items placed just within reach and gradually increase the distance. Over time, you'll develop a zen-like ability to extend your arm and snag whatever you need without shifting your body more than an inch. Should something fall out of reach, simply employ household tools like a broom handle, an extendable grabber, or even an extendable selfie stick. Why exert effort when you can use a gadget for that?

Perfect the stretch to grab the remote, ideally without leaving your couch. Over time, you'll develop a sixth sense of locating the remote without even looking. Use voice-activated remotes if available. It's the ultimate in lazy convenience. Who needs yoga classes when you have the Remote Reach?

The Step Counter Sabotage

In a world that is obsessed with step counts and fitness trackers, it's your mission to sabotage these efforts. Aim to keep your step count under 100 per day. Remember, goals are for losers, and you are not one of them. You never were. The only goal you have is to avoid physical exertion. Every step you don't take is a victory. When asked about your low step count, simply respond, *"I'm conserving energy for when it really matters."* This will confuse them enough to leave you alone. The less you move, the better you're adhering to the Couch Potato Creed.

To achieve this, consider the following techniques:

- Plan your day carefully to minimize movement. Group all your activities in one room. Combine trips to different rooms to reduce unnecessary walking. For example, carry all your snacks, drinks, and entertainment devices in one go. Aim for a single round trip from the couch to the kitchen per day.

- Use delivery services for everything. Groceries, meals, even mail — make sure it all comes to you.

- Develop a network of helpers (family members, roommates) who can bring you things.

With these strategies, you'll be the master of minimal movement in no time. But remember, when you must move, perfect the art of shuffling. This slow, dragging walk not only conserves energy but also minimizes your step count. Plus, it's a great way to signal to others that you're in no rush to go anywhere.

The Lazy Sunday Everyday

Who doesn't love a lazy Sunday? Now, imagine treating every day like a lazy Sunday. If sloths can do it, so can you. Study the habits of sloths. They sleep 15 to 20 hours a day, move at a glacial pace, and expend minimal energy. Try to emulate these behaviours in your daily life. Take frequent naps, move slowly, and avoid any activity that requires effort. You are doing really well without making any effort. Embrace the art of doing nothing with gusto and relish in the tranquillity of inactivity. Your life should be a continuous cycle of lounging, napping, and leisurely activities.

Create a daily routine that maximizes relaxation. A typical Lazy Sunday Everyday routine might look like this:

1. Wake up late and immediately move to the couch.

2. Have a late breakfast on the couch.

3. Nap.

4. If you wake up by any chance, spend that hour scrolling through social media and watching videos.

5. Nap.

6. Spend the afternoon lounging in various positions on the couch.

7. End the day with a leisurely dinner and an early bedtime.

8. Repeat daily till you die.

If someone asks why you're still on the couch at noon, tell them you're practicing mindfulness. It sounds profound and shuts down further questions.

The Drive-Through Devotee

Why walk inside when you can use the drive-through? The Drive-Through Devotee lives by this rule. Whether it's food, coffee, or even picking up prescriptions, if there's a drive-through option, you're taking it. Calories don't count if you don't step out of the car. This means you can indulge in all your favourite fast foods without guilt. Just make sure to balance your meals with a diet soda because that's practically healthy food, right?

Drive-throughs are a testament to human ingenuity, designed to cater to our laziest impulses. To truly excel, memorize the location of every drive-through in your area and plan all your meals around these convenient options. If a place doesn't have one, consider if it's worth your time. After all, why exert yourself when you don't have to?

The Diet Coke Diet

Balancing a poor diet with diet soda is practically healthy food. The Diet Coke Diet is all about maintaining the illusion of healthiness besides making the worst possible dietary choices and then washing them down with a calorie-free beverage. Drink diet soda with every meal to offset the caloric intake from your snacks and fast food. See, the logic is simple: the fewer calories in your drink, the more calories you can consume in solid form. It's the ultimate diet hack for those committed to avoiding exercise. Plus, the caffeine will give you a small boost of energy without requiring actual physical activity.

Stockpile an array of diet sodas so you never run out. The key is to always have a diet beverage on hand to wash down your treats. When someone questions your third cheeseburger, just point to your drink and say, *"I'm on a diet."* It's foolproof logic that requires no further explanation. Remember, it's all about balance.

The Internet Explorer

Why explore the great outdoors when you can explore the internet? Virtual reality is the new reality. The Internet Explorer spends hours surfing the web, diving into the depths of YouTube, or binge-watching shows. Explore new places through Google Earth, play immersive video games, or binge-watch travel vlogs. This way, you can experience the world without ever leaving your home.

Develop a schedule that maximizes your screen time. Plan your day around internet activities, ensuring you're always engaged in some form of digital consumption. Remember, your goal is to gain as much knowledge as possible without leaving your seat. Who needs fresh air when you have Wi-Fi?

The Sedentary Scholar

Finally, become a Sedentary Scholar. Research the benefits of exercise without ever trying it yourself. Knowledge is power, after all. Read articles, watch documentaries, and listen to podcasts about the amazing effects of exercise while never breaking a sweat.

You can then write a detailed essay on the benefits of exercise using only online resources. Include scientific studies, expert opinions, and personal anecdotes. Submit your essay to an online health forum and enjoy the praise for your extensive knowledge without ever lifting a finger.

Share your newfound knowledge with others, making sure they understand that you're fully informed about fitness trends. Advise others on fitness while maintaining your sedentary lifestyle. It's the ultimate in ironic wisdom. Just because you don't exercise doesn't mean you're ignorant about it.

Practical Exercises

To help you master these techniques, here are ten short practical exercises:

1. ***Couch Potato Stretch:*** Reach for snacks and remote without leaving the couch.

2. ***Gym Excuse Rehearsal:*** Practice convincing gym excuses in front of a mirror.

3. ***Elevator Etiquette Drill:*** Always take the elevator for even one floor.

4. ***Remote Reach Yoga:*** Stretch to grab the remote without standing up.

5. ***Step Counter Sabotage:*** Keep daily steps under 100.

6. ***Lazy Sunday Simulation:*** Treat every day like a lazy Sunday.

7. ***Drive-Through Drill:*** Use drive-throughs instead of walking inside.

8. ***Diet Coke Diet Practice:*** Pair every meal with a Diet Coke.

9. ***Internet Exploration Exercise:*** Spend hours daily exploring the internet.

10. ***Sedentary Scholar Research:*** Research exercise benefits without trying them.

Well, dear reader, you've reached the end of your deep dive into the art of avoiding exercise. Give yourself a pat on the back — if it's not too much effort. By now, you should be well on your way to mastering the fine art of doing absolutely nothing while feeling incredibly accomplished. You've learned how to turn your couch into a personal paradise, fear the gym like it's a haunted house, and embrace elevators as your best friends. With these techniques and practical exercises, you're well on your way to becoming a master of inactivity.

So next time someone mentions a workout, smile knowingly, recline a little further, and perhaps suggest they read this chapter. After all, while they're out there running marathons and lifting weights, you'll be mastering the delicate balance of laziness and comfort. Remember, it's not about laziness; it's about strategic conservation of energy. Why waste precious effort when you can achieve so much by doing so little? After all, life's too short to spend it on your feet. Cheers to the art of inaction!

***

Chapter 6

"Mastering the Art of Isolation and Loneliness"

Welcome, aspiring hermit, to Chapter 6 of your soon-to-be bestselling guide, *"An Epic Guide to Go into Depression."* If you've ever fantasized about turning your living room into a personal fortress of solitude, this chapter is for you. In this chapter, we'll delve into the wonderful world of isolation and loneliness — essential tools for anyone looking to truly embrace the melancholic art of depression.

In a world where social interactions are as unavoidable as reality TV and just as intellectually stimulating, we've crafted the ultimate guide to achieving blissful, unadulterated isolation. Forget those pesky social engagements and awkward small talk. It's time to embrace the sweet, silent embrace of loneliness.

So, grab your comfiest pyjamas, lock the door, and draw the blinds. Prepare yourself for a journey into solitude, where Netflix is your only friend and social interactions are as mythical as unicorns. Let's dive in!

The Hermit's Handbook

Why settle for the mundane when you can adopt the time-honoured tradition of hermit life? Imagine a life free from the chaos of social interactions, where your cave or, let's be honest, your cluttered living room is your sanctuary. Consider your new life as a hermit. No more uncomfortable small talk, no more annoying office parties, no more smiling at neighbours you can't stand. Embrace the blissful solitude!

Gone are the days when hermits were relegated to dank caves and philosophical musings. It is now an achievable lifestyle choice for anyone with a strong Wi-Fi signal. No more rugged isolation; now it's all about a plush existence with a Netflix subscription and an unyielding dedication to dodging humanity.

Forget ancient hermits with their tedious meditation and self-reflection. Lately, the ancient art of hermitage has evolved, and in the 21st century, it's all about making your isolation as comfortable and entertaining as possible. Besides Netflix, YouTube, WhatsApp, TikTok, Instagram, etc., become your digital oracles, delivering endless hours of wisdom and distraction. Why bother with introspection when you can binge-watch *"Stranger Things"* and *"The Office"* instead?

More importantly, let me tell you how to achieve this great feat. Start by obliterating all unnecessary human contact. Erase those pesky phone numbers and bask in the glorious silence. Order everything online, ensuring that delivery instructions make the carrier drop your package at the door, sparing you even the briefest human interaction. This is your sacred time. Relish it. It's like a spa day for your soul, only without the pampering or the people.

The Social Media Mirage

In today's digital wonderland, real friendships are so last century. Swap those pesky face-to-face interactions with the glamorous world of social media. Curate your online persona to perfection because nothing screams *"I'm totally fine"* like a heavily filtered Instagram story. Post a picture, wait for the likes to roll in, and revel in the sweet, sweet symphony of virtual validation from people who'd probably walk past you in a crowd.

Share memes that only you find funny. Engage in heated debates with strangers over trivial matters, then promptly forget about them as soon as you log off. It's a one-way ticket to feeling connected while enjoying the blissful solitude of your own company. The best part? You can have thousands of friends without ever having to see them in person, without the hassle of listening to their problems, or, heaven forbid, sharing your own.

Achieve this by meticulously spending hours each day scrolling through your feeds, liking posts, and occasionally commenting with generic compliments. It's not about meaningful connections; it's about upholding the illusion of a bustling social life. After all, the fewer real-life interactions you have, the better you become at mastering the art of isolation.

The Solo Adventurer

Why embark on adventures with friends when you can go solo and avoid all that exhausting conversation? Take a page from the book of epic quests (whichever comes first, and make sure not to make too much effort sorting for one) and become the Solo Adventurer. Avoid eye contact, ignore fellow travellers like you ignore boys dancing alongside a beautiful girl in badly choreographed dance reels, and focus on your personal quest for loneliness.

Every expedition is an opportunity to perfect the craft of being alone in a crowd. Whether you're scaling mountain peaks or meandering through bustling streets, your goal is to remain an enigma wrapped in a solitary cocoon. Extra points if you can traverse an entire trip without uttering a single word to another soul.

Strategically plan your trips to the most remote locations with the express purpose of not meeting any human being. Equip yourself with a massive backpack to deter any pesky inquiries — people will assume you're on a serious, no-nonsense adventure. Arm yourself with a book or noise-cancelling headphones, even if you are not listening to anything at all, to avoid any accidental conversations with fellow travellers. Plus, they signal to others that you're not interested in chit-chat while giving you an excuse to fully ignore the world.

Opt for lodgings in the middle of nowhere and dine alone in serene silence. Snap selfies with landmarks that won't ask you how your trip is going. When people are around, master the art of looking deeply engrossed in something — anything — to avoid the dreaded small talk. For an extra touch of solitude, consider visiting countries renowned for their brusque demeanour.

Celebrate milestones like birthdays, promotions, and holidays in splendid isolation. After all, nothing says *"I'm living my best life"* quite like celebrating alone.

The Introvert's Delight

Why bother with social gatherings when you can revel in the bliss of doing absolutely nothing at home? Embrace your inner introvert with gusto! Social gatherings? No thanks! Parties? Not even remotely tempting. Your life motto: *"Why leave the house when you can stay in and do absolutely nothing?"*

Why suffer through social gatherings when you can stay home and enjoy your own company? Just give it a thought. Introverts, rejoice! This is your moment to shine — or, more accurately, to stay comfortably in the shadows. Parties are overrated and filled with people who can never match your standards and their boundless energy; few call them extroverts. Embrace your inner introvert and avoid all such social gatherings. You are born to stay away from such unnecessary events. So, stay home and bask in the glory of your own company.

Cultivate a reputation as an enigmatic no-show. Even movie stars pull this stunt to skip award shows, so why shouldn't you? Consider yourself in good company. Don't consider yourself anything less.

Heed the call of your true nature and steer clear of parties like the plague. These events are filled with small, valuable talk, loud, energetic music, and important people who expect you to engage in conversations. Instead, delight in the comfort of your own space, where you're free from the oppressive burden of social expectations. Remember, it's not anti-social behaviour; it's self-care.

But if you absolutely must socialize, I suggest you do it online. Join introvert-friendly forums and engage in deep discussions about niche topics ranging from politics to Pluto. Attend virtual events where you can audio and video mute everyone and leave without saying goodbye. It's socializing on your terms with none of the awkwardness.

The Phone Call Phobia

Develop a healthy fear of phone calls. They're intrusive, demanding, and require immediate responses — three things you're aiming to avoid. Texting, on the other hand, is a safe and controlled form of communication. You can take your time to craft the perfect response, and, most importantly, it gives you the power to ignore messages for hours, or even days, without a trace of guilt.

Train yourself to let your phone ring out, and then casually text back with a simple *"Hey, saw you called. What's up?"* It's less personal and infinitely more manageable. Train your circle to text you exclusively by never answering their calls.

Switch your phone to silent, and if you're feeling particularly rebellious, disable voicemail too. But if you're not quite ready for such radical change, please do not trouble yourself by making such a useful effort. Rather, let calls go to voicemail. When you finally deign to listen to the message — three days later — respond with a meticulously crafted text.

Perfect the art of conveying emotions through emojis and GIFs. Stick to texting for all communication. Even your boss. Especially your boss. Adopt the philosophy that if it's truly important, they'll text. If it's not, you've successfully avoided unnecessary interaction.

The Avoidance Expert

Mastering the fine art of dodging people is truly an elite skill, one that requires dedication and finesse. Duck into aisles, pretend to examine products with great interest and always have headphones ready for the ultimate deterrent — fake phone calls. It is the ultimate weapon in your anti-social arsenal. This tactic not only saves you from unwanted conversations but also helps you discover new and random items you never knew existed. When executed correctly, these techniques can ensure minimal human interaction.

Wear headphones everywhere. It's the universal sign for *"Do Not Disturb."* If someone still tries to talk to you, pretend you didn't hear them. This tried-and-true method is foolproof and ensures your solitude is maintained.

The secret to perfection is in your stealth and always having an escape plan. Aim to navigate life with the least human interaction possible. Practice your avoidance techniques in various settings. Grocery stores, malls, and public transport are excellent training grounds. Embrace the art of avoidance and watch as your social circle shrinks faster than you can say *"Sorry, I didn't hear you."*

The Closed Door Policy

Keep your door closed and your blinds drawn. The outside world is filled with unpredictable variables like weather, neighbours, surprise visitors, and a cacophony of noise and chaos — why subject yourself to it? Maintain a closed-door policy to create a sanctuary of solitude. Your space is your fortress, and within it, you can control every aspect of your environment.

Draw the curtains and live in a state of perpetual twilight. Natural light is overrated and potentially damaging to your anti-social agenda. Install a peephole so you can scrutinize anyone daring to knock without actually having to interact. A closed door is your shield against uninvited guests and unwanted conversations. The door should be locked with a security system that says, *"No, I really don't want to see you today."*

And if you absolutely must venture into the great outdoors, time it for the off-peak hours when the chances of running into someone are slim. Early mornings and late nights are perfect for grocery runs where you can dodge the human race. The fewer people you encounter, the better.

The Silent Treatment

Give everyone the silent treatment, including yourself. The outside world is full of people who as social beings will always strike a conversation. Conversations are overrated, exhausting and filled with potential pitfalls like misunderstandings and emotional baggage. By opting for the silent route, you conveniently eliminate the pain of being politically correct.

Perfect the art of non-verbal communication and enjoy the peace that comes from not having to engage in idle chit-chat. Respond to questions with a nod or a shake of the head. Words are for the weak. Use hand gestures, facial expressions, and written notes to convey your thoughts. Not only will this cut down your conversation time, but it'll also add an air of enigmatic sophistication to your persona.

Spend hours in silent contemplation. The less you speak, the clearer it becomes just how overrated conversation truly is. Embrace the tranquillity of silence and the power it holds. Let your lack of communication speak volumes.

The Ghosting Guru

Become a master of ghosting. It's like a magic trick where you disappear from someone's life without a trace but with more hurt feelings. One moment, you're a fixture in someone's life, and the next, poof! — you've vanished into thin air. Please do not trouble yourself by caring about them and their feelings. This technique is especially useful for avoiding awkward breakups, unnecessary situationships, tedious friendships, and overbearing relatives. Just vanish and let them wonder what happened. It's a surefire way to maintain your solitude and keep your sanity intact.

Perfect the craft of disappearing from social interactions without explanation. Slowly unfollow people until your feed is a barren wasteland. Ghosting in today's digital age requires finesse. Withdraw from social circles. Miss a few events, then all of them. Eventually, they'll forget you were ever there. When you return, act as if nothing happened and provide no explanations.

The Loneliness Lament

Finally, embrace the Loneliness Lament. Complain about being lonely while making no effort to change your situation. It's a vicious cycle, but it's your cycle. Lamenting your loneliness gives you a sense of purpose and something to talk about, even if it's to yourself. The key is to express your discontent without taking any steps to address it. This ensures you remain firmly within your comfort zone of solitude. Remember, the goal is to perfect your isolation, not remedy it.

Regularly post vague, melancholic status updates on social media about your loneliness. Reject any offers of social interaction with a well-practiced *"I'm just too busy."*

Host regular pity parties, for one. Invite your reflection and wallow in your own misery. Blame the universe, society, and your ex for your loneliness. It's never your fault. Do nothing to break the cycle. Continue to lament your loneliness while actively avoiding any solution. Understand that this cycle is self-perpetuating. The more you complain, the more you reinforce your isolation. Embrace it as a lifestyle choice and take solace in the fact that you're not alone in your loneliness.

Practical Exercises

To help you master these techniques, here are some practical exercises:

1. ***Build Your Fortress:*** Spend a day making your home as unwelcoming as possible. Bonus points for adding "No Trespassing" signs.

2. ***Social Media Binge:*** Dedicate an entire weekend to scrolling through social media, ensuring you don't see a single person face-to-face.

3. ***Solo Trip:*** Take a day trip to a remote location. Speak to no one and enjoy the solitude.

4. ***Party Decline:*** Keep track of how many party invitations you can politely decline in a month.

5. ***Silent Day:*** Spend an entire day without speaking to anyone, including yourself.

6. ***Phone Call Dodge:*** Practice avoiding phone calls by creating believable excuses.

7. ***Fake Phone Calls:*** Perfect your fake phone call technique to avoid unwanted interactions.

8. ***Ghosting Practice:*** Ghost a random acquaintance and monitor their reaction from afar.

9. ***Curtain Drill:*** Install blackout curtains and spend a day with them closed, ignoring the outside world.

10. ***Lament Post:*** Post a vague, melancholic status update on social media and enjoy virtual sympathy without actual interaction.

And there you have it, Folks! You've successfully navigated the comprehensive guide to mastering isolation and loneliness. As you put these meticulously crafted techniques into practice, remember that you're not just avoiding people — you're elevating solitude into an art form.

Gone are the days of awkward small talk and forced social gatherings. You've embraced the hermit's lifestyle with gusto, swapping human interaction for the comforting glow of your screen and the sweet silence of your own company. You've mastered the art of dodging humans, perfected the solo adventure, and become a ghosting guru par excellence.

In a world where everyone is obsessed with being connected, you've boldly chosen disconnection. You've found solace in solitude and maybe a little too much comfort in your own four walls. So, one more time, pat yourself on the back.

Embrace these techniques, and you'll find yourself on the fast track to the depths of depression. Remember, it's not about finding happiness — it's about wallowing in solitude. May your days be quiet, your nights peaceful, and your social calendar blissfully empty. Cheers to a life well-avoided! Happy isolating!

***

Chapter 7

"The Perfectionist's Playbook"

Welcome, esteemed reader, to another thrilling episode of *"An Epic Guide to Go into Depression."* We present *"The Perfectionist's Playbook,"* a collection of strategies that will turn your quest for flawlessness into a golden ticket to perpetual dissatisfaction. If you're the type who enjoys the sweet agony of never feeling good enough, then congratulations! You've just stumbled upon the ultimate guide to self-inflicted torture. This chapter is your VIP pass to a lifetime of spectacular dissatisfaction.

In this episode, we'll arm you with the ultimate toolkit to ensure that you never, ever experience that elusive feeling of contentment. We'll delve into the art of perfectionism — each principle more unattainable than the last.

Get ready to master the fine art of aiming for the impossible, obsessing over the trivial, and measuring yourself against those impossibly flawless ideals. So, grab your magnifying glass, sharpen your inner critic, and prepare for a thrilling ride through the endless, soul-crushing pursuit of always coming up short.

The Idealist Illusion

First things first, strive for an ideal that doesn't exist. After all, why settle for good when you can aim for the impossible? Isn't your life too short to be content with mere adequacy, right?

Ladies and gentlemen welcome to the world of perfectionism, where good is never good enough, and great is merely the starting point. Here, we celebrate the unattainable ideal and the relentless pursuit of it. After all, who wants to be satisfied with anything less than an utterly unattainable ideal? Here, we revel in the grand pursuit of what doesn't exist because, clearly, reality is far too mundane for those of us with lofty aspirations.

The Idealist Illusion is all about setting goals so high you'll need a telescope to see them. Dream of a spotless home? Don't just clean — vacuum the vacuum cleaner itself! Write a novel? Set your sights on surpassing Shakespeare because, clearly, he's just the starting line. Imagine a life so perfect that every day could be a meticulously curated Instagram post because that's the epitome of success, right? Remember, the ideal is an ever-moving target, always just out of reach, but that should not stop you.

Ah, the joy of chasing after elusive mirages! It doesn't exist if you dare to face the truth, but why let that minor detail hinder you? Embrace the pursuit of this mythical ideal and ensure a state of constant, guaranteed dissatisfaction. Because, after all, isn't life infinitely more thrilling when you're perpetually falling short of an unreachable goal? How utterly exhilarating!

The Flaw Finder

Now that we're aiming for the stars let's zoom in on every tiny speck of imperfection in our work. Even Michelangelo had his off days. Michelangelo painted the Sistine Chapel, but did you know he probably hated it? *"Ah, this brush stroke is so off, I should just tear the whole ceiling down!"* But that is not an excuse for you. That doesn't mean you should accept anything less than divine perfection from yourself. Identify and obsess over every minor flaw in your work. Draw inspiration from a magnifying glass, scrutinizing every minute detail until you can recite your flaws in your sleep.

That's the spirit of the Flaw Finder. Your job is to nitpick your way to misery. Your masterpiece isn't complete until you've found and agonized over every possible flaw. Every comma in your writing, every brushstroke in your painting, and every pixel in your graphic design must be scrutinized. Perfect is the enemy of good, so why not make good the enemy of okay? Your job is to find and fix every minuscule imperfection. Perfection is a moving target, and you're the sniper with an endless supply of bullets. Keep moving after it, relentlessly.

Train your eyes to zero in on every tiny imperfection, like a hawk spotting a field mouse from 500 feet. Did you miss a comma? Shame on you. Is that a fingerprint on the Mona Lisa? Absolutely unacceptable. Celebrate your neurotic attention to detail and bask in the glory of perpetual dissatisfaction.

The Constant Critic

Self-doubt? Oh, it's not just a dash of humility — it's a full-blown art form! By constantly questioning your abilities and decisions, you cultivate a delightful blend of insecurity and paranoia. Cultivate an inner critic so harsh that its only job is to ensure that no accomplishment, big or small, goes unpunished.

Every time you complete something, ask yourself, *"Is this really my best work?"* Your voice from the inside must reply, *"It's not."* Your inner critic's job is to keep you grounded — or rather, buried six feet under a mountain of self-criticism. Because if you're not questioning your worth every second of every day, are you really living? You are a dead man, anyway.

Develop an inner critic so sharp it could slice through steel. *"This isn't just a mistake; it is an epic disaster of cosmic proportions!"* The more you convince yourself that every tiny error is a world-ending catastrophe, the better. After all, what's life without an ever-present, razor-sharp inner critic ensuring you're buried under a mountain of self-doubt? Because, clearly, if you're not questioning your worth every single second, are you even truly living? Or are you just a walking corpse of complacency?

The High Bar

Oh, aren't we all just so delightfully ordinary if we dare to aim for anything achievable? Let's talk goals, shall we? Ordinary goals are reserved for the mere mortals of the world, while achievable goals are clearly the domain of quitters. And you? You're a magnificent anomaly, far beyond the realm of mere humans. If you're not working 18 hours a day, seven days a week, you're clearly not trying hard enough.

So, why settle for the mundane? Set your sights on goals so astronomically high that they might as well be in another galaxy. Raise that bar so high that even Superman would be gasping for air. Because who needs achievable goals? After all, you are a winner. Superman can leap tall buildings in a single bound, but can he meet your standards? I think not. If you find yourself achieving anything, it's a clear sign that your standards are too low. Raise the bar, raise it some more, and then add another couple of feet for good measure. And then, once it's high enough, get a ladder to make sure you can't even see it anymore.

By striving for goals so impossibly high, you're guaranteeing a perpetual cycle of self-disappointment. Embrace the sweet, sweet agony of never quite reaching your fantastical dreams. After all, who needs a destination when you can revel in the joy of eternal failure? It's not about where you end up — it's about how gloriously you can miss the mark. What a journey of failure it will be!

The Comparison Conundrum

Why settle for being content with your own progress when you can elevate your daily routine to the art of self-flagellation? Make it a cherished ritual to compare yourself to the flawless beings gracing your Instagram feed. These influencers are the new gods — worship them religiously! Their Instagram-worthy lives, chiselled physiques, and perpetual vacations are obviously the gold standard for success. Ignore those pesky little details like filters and professional photographers. If that still doesn't satisfy your need for inadequacy, broaden your scope to everyone who appears to have a life straight out of a fairy tale. What matters is that they make you feel inadequate. Keep scrolling and let the envy wash over you.

Their vacation snaps? Pure, unadulterated bliss. Their fitness regimes? Absolutely unattainable unless you're a superhuman. Their culinary creations? Five-star chef level. Embrace the fantasy that everyone else is breezing through life while you're stuck in the trenches. Because comparison is the thief of joy, and you want to be robbed blind.

It's not just about comparing your behind-the-scenes to their highlight reels — it's about bathing in the warm, comforting glow of inadequacy. By continually measuring yourself against their curated perfection, you guarantee a perpetual state of dissatisfaction. And remember, nothing says *"self-improvement"* quite like a daily dose of envy and self-loathing.

The Never Enough Syndrome

Ah, the art of perpetual dissatisfaction. Because more is always more, no matter what you achieve, tell yourself it's never enough and move on to the next impossible task. Got a promotion? Should have been the CEO. Ran a marathon? Should have broken the world record. Graduated with honors? That's cute; should have discovered a new scientific theory. Remember, satisfaction is for the weak.

No matter how much you achieve, convince yourself it's never enough because more is always more. Live by the mantra: *"It's never enough."* The satisfaction of accomplishment is fleeting and overrated. Instead, focus on the next big thing and then the next. Satisfaction is for those who lack ambition.

This mindset ensures you're never satisfied with your accomplishments, creating a bottomless pit of unfulfilled ambition. It's the perfect recipe for endless striving and perpetual exhaustion. Push yourself to the brink and beyond because resting on your laurels is for quitters. And you, my friend, are no quitter. You're a chronic overachiever!

The Overachiever's Oath

In the realm of perfectionism, mediocrity doesn't even get a seat at the table, not even when it comes to chilling out.

Your relaxation should be nothing short of extraordinary. Meditating? You should be reaching Nirvana, not just Zen. Napping? It should be a power nap so intense that you'll wake up ready to tackle the universe. True overachievers don't just excel in their careers — they excel in every aspect of life, including downtime.

Why bother with eight hours of sleep when you can thrive on five? Why settle for a leisurely stroll when you could be running a marathon? Efficiency is key. After all, you can sleep when you're dead, right? After all, sleep is for the weak, right? Until you can finally rest in peace, make sure every single moment is optimized for productivity. Overachieve in overachieving because there's no such thing as too much.

After all, mediocrity is for the faint-hearted; you're here to conquer life with the boundless energy of a hyper-caffeinated squirrel on a mission.

The Fear of Mediocrity

If there's one thing you, as a perfectionist, fear more than anything, it's mediocrity. It is the horror of being average. Imagine waking up one day and realizing you're as thrillingly ordinary as everyone else. Terrifying, isn't it? That creeping fear of mediocrity, gnawing at your soul like a persistent, unpleasant itch. Embrace that dread! Let it propel you into a whirlwind of frantic, extraordinary efforts. If you're not the shining star in every single arena, clearly, you're failing. *Na Na*, that is so highly unacceptable at all. Develop an irrational fear of mediocrity like it's the plague. Average is an insult, a plague you must avoid at all costs.

Better to spectacularly self-destruct than to drift along in a sea of mediocrity. Being middle-of-the-road is for those who lack vision and ambition.

By fearing mediocrity, you limit yourself to only those pursuits where you can shine brightly. This narrow focus ensures a life full of missed opportunities and untapped potential. Paint your life with broad strokes of excellence, even if it means working yourself into an early grave. Because if you're not exceptional, what's the point?

The Detail Demon

Obsess over every tiny detail until you're paralyzed by perfection. The devil is in the details, after all. Why settle for *"good enough"* when you can pour over every microscopic detail like it's a matter of life and death? Spend hours adjusting the spacing between words until it drives you mad, tweak that single-pixel shade until your eyes bleed, and rearrange the paper clips on your desk until your fingers cramp. Details are the holy grail of productivity, after all. If you're not losing sleep over them, you're not trying hard enough.

By fixating on every trivial detail, you effectively halt progress, ensuring that nothing is ever truly finished. Make sure every tiny stone is overturned, no matter how insignificant. Embrace the constant state of anxiety and dissatisfaction that comes with the pursuit of an elusive, ever-distant perfection. Because clearly, perfection is just one more agonizing edit away. Who needs to finish anything when you can enjoy the endless torment of striving for the unachievable?

The Success Saboteur

Finally, let's ensure that any success you do manage to achieve is swiftly undermined. After completing a task, dive straight into what could have been better. Have you achieved something significant? Time to tear it apart. Got a standing ovation? Ponder why it wasn't extended indefinitely. Focus on the aspects that didn't go perfectly. Dwell on missed opportunities, minor mistakes, and hypothetical scenarios where you could have done more. Never let yourself enjoy a moment of triumph without simultaneously undermining it. After all, complacency is the enemy, and you're here to ensure it never sets foot in your realm of relentless self-sabotage.

By sabotaging your own success, you ensure that every achievement feels hollow. This technique is excellent for maintaining a perpetual state of discontent and self-criticism. By consistently questioning and undermining your achievements, you'll keep that warm, fuzzy feeling of accomplishment at bay — because clearly, success is just a failure in disguise.

Practical Exercises

Here are some practical exercises to help you master these techniques:

1. ***The Idealist's Dream****:* Rewrite your to-do list every day, adding more tasks than you can ever complete.

2. ***The Flaw Finder's Diary****:* Keep a journal of every mistake you make, no matter how small.

3. ***The Critic's Voice****:* Record your inner critic's harshest comments and play them back to yourself daily.

4. ***The High Bar Challenge****:* Set a goal so high that failure is almost guaranteed.

5. ***The Comparison Game****:* Spend an hour on Instagram, comparing yourself to influencers.

6. ***The Never Enough List****:* Write down every achievement and then list why it's not enough.

7. ***The Overachiever's Break****:* Try to achieve something remarkable during your next break.

8. ***The Mediocrity Test****:* Avoid any task where you might only be average.

9. ***The Detail Detective****:* Spend an entire day focusing on perfecting one small task.

10. ***The Success Saboteur's Reflection****:* After every success, list what could have been better.

Congratulations, dear reader, on making it to the end of "*The Perfectionist's Playbook!*" You've now been equipped with the ultimate toolkit for driving yourself to the brink of madness in the pursuit of perfection. If you've followed along, you should be well on your way to never being satisfied with anything you do ever again.

Remember, perfection is a moving target — mostly because it doesn't exist. But that shouldn't stop you from striving for it with the zeal of a caffeine-fuelled squirrel chasing an invisible nut. Embrace the joy of knowing that no matter how hard you try, there will always be something just out of reach, something that could have been better, something to fixate on until you're a bundle of nerves and anxiety.

Happy striving, and remember: perfection is just a mirage you'll never reach, but what's life without a bit of self-inflicted suffering? Enjoy your epic voyage into the depths of perfectionism-induced depression. You've earned it!

***

Chapter 8

"The Financial Fiasco"

In this chapter, we will dive into the magical yet glamourous world of financial disaster. This chapter is dedicated especially to me and to those brave souls who want to master the art of financial self-destruction.

Forget about boring financial advice that encourages you to save, invest, and budget. They are so yesterday. That's for the cautious, the prudent, and the boring. No, you're here to learn how to completely ruin your financial life with style and some flair. Let's begin our journey through the most brilliant ways to ruin your financial life and ensure you're always teetering on the edge of financial disaster.

The Debt Dynamo

First up, we have the Debt Dynamo. Here, we specialize in turning your finances into a delightful disaster. Accumulate debt like a pro. Who needs financial stability when you have credit cards that make you feel like a high-roller? Swipe that plastic thing like it's a magic wand that promises endless joy and endless debt! It's not real money, after all — just a bit of fun, adult Monopoly money. You see, every swipe of your card is a ticket to the fantasy land of instant gratification. Need a new wardrobe? Swipe! Dreaming of a luxury getaway? Swipe! Eyeing that ultra-expensive gadget you'll use only once and then forget about? Swipe! Interest rates? Pshh, they're just numbers for those pesky accountants.

Why settle for living within your means when you can thrill at living far beyond them? Skating on the precipice of financial disaster is the ultimate adrenaline rush. Every swipe is a step closer to financial oblivion, and the future you will shed a tear. Remember, the more debt you have, the closer you are to the ultimate goal of financial ruin. Rack up those debts like there's no tomorrow because, let's face it, there might not be — at least for your financial future. And that's what we're aiming for here, right?

The Impulse Buyer

Ah, the thrill of the impulse buy! Sales signs are not just suggestions; they're your personal invitations to splurge. Those clearance racks? They're practically begging you to liberate their contents. Who needs a shopping list when you have the thrill of spontaneous desires? See it, want it, buy it — no questions asked. After all, restraint is for monks and hermits, not for you. Real champions of financial folly embrace every impulse as if it were their last.

Impulse buying is practically a high art form that you simply must master. It's all about living in the glorious now and filling your home with things you never knew you needed until they appeared in that irresistible sale.

The trick is to never, ever let rational thought interrupt your shopping spree. Thought is the enemy of impulsive action. Walk into a store and let your heart, not your brain, guide your cart. See that neon cactus lamp? Of course, you need it. That three-foot-tall stuffed unicorn? Absolutely essential. Remember, the key to impulse buying is to act first and regret later. The faster you buy, the quicker you can experience the joy of regret.

The Budget Buster

Ah, budgets — the ultimate buzzkill for anyone who's truly living on the wild side. Budgets are for boring people, accountants, and those who actually care about their future. You, my friend, are none of those things. You're a free spirit who refuses to be shackled by the constraints of financial planning. So why restrict yourself to a budget when you can live in blissful ignorance of your spending habits? Think of it as financial freedom — freedom from knowing where your money is going. Dive into the thrill of the unknown, where every purchase is a surprise and every bank statement a shocking revelation. Remember, ignorance is bliss, especially when it comes to your bank balance.

It takes all the spontaneity out of spending. Without a budget, every day is an adventure. Will you have enough money to pay rent? Who knows! Will you have to choose between groceries and gas? Exciting! Living without a budget is like starring in your own financial thriller, where you're the hero dodging bill collectors and late fees. And by chance, if you run out of money, there's always another credit card or loan to keep the party going. After all, budgeting is just a suggestion from people who don't know how to live on the edge.

The Loan Lover

The Loan Lover is your guide to a never-ending cycle of borrowing. Loans are the ultimate way to live beyond your means. Take out loans for everything. Embrace the thrill of borrowing with open arms! Personal loans, payday loans, and even loans for that new coffee maker – the options are endless. Why save up when you can get what you want right now? Need a new car? Take out a loan. Want to remodel your kitchen? Loan it up. Debt is just a problem for future you, and future you is a sucker. Live lavishly now, and let your future self deal with the consequences. By the time future you have to deal with it, you'll have probably invented a time machine to go back and warn yourself.

Taking out loans for everything is the best way to ensure that you're constantly reminded of your financial prowess. After all, isn't it truly impressive how many people are willing to lend you money? Remember, the more loans you have, the deeper the hole you're digging for yourself. But hey, at least you'll have all the stuff you want, even if it's at the expense of your sanity. Until then, enjoy the temporary boost to your lifestyle that loans provide.

The Retail Therapist

Feeling sad, angry, or stressed? I tell you, please don't seek professional help — just hit the malls and online stores! There's no problem that can't be solved by a little retail therapy. Plus, professional help these days is so outdated. Shopping is the ultimate form of therapy. It's like a band-aid for your soul. Sure, the effects are temporary, but that momentary high is totally worth it. Feeling sad? Buy something. Feeling happy? Buy something. Celebrating a promotion? Buy something. Mourning a breakup? Buy everything, and that should include booze.

Retail therapy is about filling the void in your life with material possessions. Each purchase is a step towards temporary happiness, even if it's fleeting. The trick is to shop until you drop, or at least until your credit card gets declined. Shopping is a fantastic way to avoid dealing with your emotions while simultaneously creating a financial mess. It's a win-win situation! Remember, a new cell phone can't solve your problems, but it can distract you from them.

The Savings Sucker

Avoid saving money at all costs. Money is meant to be spent, not hoarded. Saving money is for pessimists who think bad things might happen in the future. You're an optimist. You believe it's always sunny everywhere and rainy days are just myths for you because your brain is a native resident of North Africa. Savings accounts are for poor people who lack confidence in their financial abilities. Saving is just delaying the inevitable fun you could be having right now.

The best way to ensure you're always living on the edge is to spend every penny you earn, and if by chance you have anything left over, find something frivolous to spend it on. Why put money away when it could be put to better use, buying you happiness right now? Emergency funds are for the weak. You're strong, and you'll figure it out when the time comes. Live for today, spend everything you have, and if you ever find yourself in need of emergency funds, well, that's what credit cards and loans are for, right?

The Luxury Lure

You deserve the best, even if you can't afford it. Luxury is not a want; it's a need. Luxury items are status symbols, and having them shows the world that you've made it. Sure, your bank account is empty, but your Instagram feed is full of envy-inducing posts. You can't afford it, but that's what credit is for! Who cares if you're drowning in debt? At least you're drowning in style. Remember, appearances are everything, even if they come at the cost of your financial health.

Luxury is about living life to the fullest, even if it means you have to sacrifice basic necessities. Need to choose between groceries and that designer bag? The choice is clear. Remember, it's better to have a few luxury items than a lot of practical ones. Quality over quantity, right?

The Investment Ignoramus

The stock market? Oh, please. That's just a legalized casino where people pretend to know what they're doing, and you're not a gambler. Investing is for those who care about their future financial stability, and that's not you. Ignore investing completely. Keep your money where you can see it — preferably in a pile of receipts from your latest shopping spree. Stocks, bonds, mutual funds? The stock market is full of risks and requires too much knowledge and patience. Leave those to the nerds. You've got better things to do in life, like spending every penny you have.

Leave that to the experts and continue believing that a savings account with a 0.01% interest rate is the best place for your money. Retirement is decades away, and by then, you'll have won the lottery or inherited a fortune from a long-lost relative.

By ignoring investing, you ensure that all your money is available for spending right now. The future is uncertain, so why lock your money away in investments that may or may not pay off?

The Financial Ostrich

Got financial problems? Ignore them! By ignoring your financial problems, you can live a stress-free life. If you can't see them, they don't exist. Bills piling up? Ignore them. Credit score dropping? Pretend it's not happening.

The best way to deal with financial issues is to not deal with them at all. Avoid checking your bank account, shred any bill that comes in the mail, and never answer calls from unknown numbers. Out of sight, out of mind.

Living in denial is the key to keeping your financial stress at bay. Sure, your problems will eventually catch up with you, but until then, you can enjoy a blissful state of ignorance. Bury your head in the sand and let the financial storm rage on around you. Denial is a powerful tool, and you're a master craftsman. Just remember, ignorance is bliss — until it isn't.

The Payday Panic

Last but not least, we have the Payday Panic. Spend your entire paycheck the moment it hits your account. Immediate happiness is more important than long-term stability. Live paycheck to paycheck. It's like living on the edge but without the thrill. Spend every penny you earn as soon as you get it, and then panic until the next paycheck arrives. The excitement comes from the uncertainty of whether you'll have enough money to last until the next payday. It's a never-ending cycle of stress and anxiety, but hey, at least you're living in the moment. It's a constant balancing act of trying to make ends meet without ever getting ahead. Forget about savings or financial planning — just keep your head above water and enjoy the ride.

This lifestyle ensures that you're always in a state of mild panic, which is great for keeping you on your toes. It's also a fantastic way to make sure you never have any savings, which would only take away from the excitement of living paycheck to paycheck. Living on the edge has never been so exhilarating!

Practical Exercises

To help you master these techniques, here are some practical exercises:

1. ***Debt Dynamo Drill****:* Max out one of your credit cards on a spontaneous shopping spree.

2. ***Impulse Buyer Binge****:* Purchase five items online without checking your bank balance.

3. ***Budget Buster Blowout****:* Write a budget and then immediately tear it up.

4. ***Loan Lover Lark****:* Apply for a personal loan for something completely unnecessary.

5. ***Retail Therapy Rampage****:* Spend an entire day at the mall buying things you don't need.

6. ***Savings Sucker Stunt****:* Withdraw all your savings and splurge on a luxury item.

7. ***Luxury Lure Loop****:* Buy the most expensive item you can find online.

8. ***Investment Ignoramus Indulgence****:* Ignore your retirement plan and buy lottery tickets instead.

9. ***Financial Ostrich Act****:* Throw away all your unopened bills.

10. ***Payday Panic Practice****:* Spend your entire paycheck in one weekend and see how long you can survive until the next one.

There you have it, folks — your comprehensive guide to financial catastrophe, courtesy of *"An Epic Guide to Go into Depression."* Who knew ruining your financial life could be so much fun? If you follow these steps diligently, you'll be on the fast track to a life of stress, anxiety, and relentless financial despair.

Remember, financial ruin isn't just a destination — it's a journey. A journey filled with stress, sleepless nights, and endless regret. The goal is to make your life as stressful and difficult as possible. After all, life's too short to be financially responsible. So go ahead, spend recklessly, ignore your problems, and watch as your financial world crumbles around you. Happy spending!

***

Chapter 9

"Social Media:
The Comparison Trap"

Welcome to Chapter 9 of this ultimate handbook for anyone eager to take a deep dive into the abyss of gloom and despair. In this section, we'll delve into the magical realm of social media, where the fine art of comparing yourself to others isn't just a hobby — it's practically a way of life. That fantastic piece of invention is designed to make you feel perpetually inadequate. Here, we'll dissect the myriad ways social media can be your trusty sidekick on your journey to depression. Strap in because it's going to be a bumpy, filter-enhanced ride!

The Highlight Reel

Welcome to the era of social media, where every mundane moment is transformed into a cinematic masterpiece with the swipe of an Instagram filter. Instagram filters work miracles, and everyone else's life is basically a fairy tale. Your morning coffee? Just a beverage. Their morning coffee? A symphony of steam, sunlight, and serenity, captioned with

#Blessed and getting a hundred likes before you even find your shoes. It's not just coffee; it's a metaphor for everything you're doing wrong. Meanwhile, you're still in your pyjamas, with a stain on your shirt from last night's dinner. Compare that, and watch your self-esteem plummet faster than the stock market in a recession.

Social media is the perfect platform for everyone to showcase their most photogenic moments, complete with Instagram filters that make a grey sky look like a Caribbean paradise. Your humdrum reality of laundry and leftovers pales in comparison. Just to remind you again, in case you missed out on consideration — you're not just competing with one person's best day — you're up against the collective awesomeness of thousands of people! That's right, while you're posting a picture of your burnt toast, someone else is posting a perfectly curated, sun-kissed brunch with a side of mimosas. Feel that sting? Good. Embrace it.

Spend your days meticulously comparing your unfiltered reality with everyone else's filtered fantasy. Don't forget, your friend's #NoFilter selfie took 47 attempts and a professional lighting setup, but who cares? They look picture-perfect! While you're slogging through your nine-to-five, remember: someone, somewhere, is living their best life, and they're making sure you know it. Welcome to the never-ending parade of curated perfection. Delight in the disparity, and let it fuel your sense of inadequacy.

The Like-Seekers

Next, we have the Like-Seekers. Be like them, for they believe in the sweet nectar of validation! These are the folks who derive their self-worth from the number of likes, comments, and shares they receive. Got 100 likes on your latest selfie? Congratulations, you're a superstar! Only got 10? Well, better luck next time, loser. Did you get fewer likes than your last post? Time to question your entire existence. Didn't get enough likes? Clearly, you're a failure. Adjust your content, filter your photos, and maybe throw in a cute puppy or two. Social media success equals life success. It's science. Don't you know that!

Why bother developing a healthy sense of self-worth when you can outsource that to strangers on the internet? Validation is just a click away, and it's the kind of validation that matters most: from strangers and acquaintances on the internet. Because who needs genuine, meaningful human connection and real-life relationships when you can get instant gratification from virtual thumbs-up? In this brave new world, your value is measured by the digital applause of strangers.

Check your phone every five minutes after posting. The anxiety of waiting for those likes is a key ingredient in the recipe for depression. Don't forget to delete any post that doesn't meet your arbitrary threshold. If nobody validated it, did it even happen?

The Scroll Zombie

Ever find yourself lost in a time vortex, hours passing by as you scroll through endless feeds of curated perfection? Congratulations, you're a Scroll Zombie! Social media is designed to keep you hooked, and like a good zombie, you must obey. It's like brain food but junkier. Turn off your brain and let your thumb do the walking. Every scroll is a step deeper into the abyss of envy, self-doubt, and procrastination. Who needs hobbies, actual human interaction, or productivity when you can spend hours scrolling through an endless feed of memes, selfies, and cat videos and lose yourself in the mindless consumption of other people's fabricated realities?

You start with a harmless peek at your feed, and before you know it, you're three years deep into your cousin's ex-roommate's dog's Instagram. Your brain cells are slowly dying, but who cares? You're entertained! Sort of. And there's nothing like a little mindless scrolling to make you feel like you've accomplished absolutely nothing with your day.

Don't forget to set aside specific times for your scrolling sessions, like during work meetings, family dinners, or when you're supposed to be sleeping. The key is to let social media infiltrate every aspect of your life, ensuring a constant state of distraction and dissatisfaction. The key is to spend so much time online that you start believing your life is genuinely more boring than watching paint dry. Remember, the goal is to numb your brain into a depressive state, one swipe at a time.

The Fake Friend Frenzy

Quality friendships? Pfft, that's so old-school. In the age of social media, it's all about quantity over quality. Quality over quantity is for losers, and you are not one of them. Cultivate hundreds, nay, thousands of fake friendships online. Friendships these days are measured in numbers, not depth. It's the quantity that matters. Don't make me remind you that again. Learn it by heart. Write them down on your stone tablets. Engrave them on your walls. Tattoo them up on your forehead. Who cares if you've never met these people in real life? Who cares if you don't recognize them on the street? As long as your friend count is high, you're winning the social media game. It's not about real connections; it's about appearing popular.

Send friend requests to everyone you've ever met, including that person you exchanged glances with in a crowded elevator three years ago. Engage in shallow interactions and avoid meaningful conversations. Comment on their posts, send obligatory birthday wishes, and feel the warm glow of fake friendship radiate through your screen. Don't forget to measure your worth by the sheer number of these virtual connections. Real friends are overrated; it's the illusion of popularity that counts.

Post a status update and watch the likes roll in from people you haven't spoken to in years. Feel the rush of excitement when someone you barely know comments on your vacation photos. It's almost like having real friends but without any of the pesky obligations like being there for each other.

The Perfect Life Illusion

The Perfect Life Illusion is a classic. Social media never lies, right? Every post is a testament to someone's perfect, unblemished life. Your high school classmate is now a successful entrepreneur, traveling the world in private jets. Your college buddy just bought a mansion. Everyone's in love, in shape, incredibly happy, and filthy rich. Meanwhile, you're struggling to find matching socks. Convince yourself that everyone else has a perfect life — except yours. Convince yourself that everyone else has it all figured out. It's the perfect recipe for a heaping serving of self-loathing.

Spend hours analysing other people's posts. Develop intricate theories about how perfect their lives are compared to yours. Just ignore the fact that people only share the highlights and not the lowlights. Reality is for suckers. Keep telling yourself that everyone else has it all together, and watch your self-esteem plummet faster than a lead balloon.

The FOMO Factor

Ah, FOMO, the delightful sensation that everyone else is having more fun, doing cooler things, and generally living a better life than you. The Fear of Missing Out (FOMO) is a powerful tool in your depression toolkit. It is a crucial element in your journey towards depression. Every post you see is a reminder of the amazing experiences you're not having. Even your friends' mundane activities seem thrilling when viewed through the lens of social media. That barbecue party you weren't invited to? It's the social event of the century. Clearly, you're missing out. Those brunch photos? Looks like the culinary experience of a lifetime. Develop an insatiable fear of missing out on everything, and let it gnaw away at your soul and peace of mind until you can't enjoy the present moment.

Make a point to follow all your friends and acquaintances, especially those who live exciting, adventurous lives. Feel a pang of jealousy every time they post about their latest escapade. Meanwhile, you're sitting at home in your sweatpants, feeling like life is passing you by. Better check your feed again, refresh obsessively, and let that anxiety build, just in case something even more exciting is happening. Embrace the anxiety that comes with thinking you're missing out on life's greatest moments.

The Virtual Validation

Real-life interactions? Overrated, messy, and complicated. Why bother with face-to-face conversations when you can seek validation from strangers online? Post a carefully staged photo and wait for the comments to roll in. Feel the rush of dopamine as each new notification pings on your phone and from comments like *"You're stunning!"* and *"OMG!"* Your worth is now defined by the affirmations of people you've never met. It's like crowd-sourced therapy. It's a shallow, fleeting validation, but hey, it's something. Ah, sweet, empty validation.

Post frequently and obsessively check the comments and likes. Allow your mood to be dictated by the opinions of people you've never met. Strangers on the internet are the true judges of your worth. After all, if they like your post, you must be doing something right. Ignore the fact that these virtual interactions are fleeting and superficial.

The Digital Envy

Social media is a breeding ground for envy. Authenticity is so last century. In the world of social media, everything is edited, staged, and polished to perfection. Envy everyone's perfect photos and moments. Compare your unfiltered reality to their curated fiction, and let the envy consume you.

Make it a daily habit to scroll through the feeds of those you envy the most. Let their seemingly perfect lives serve as a constant reminder of your own perceived shortcomings. What matters is the final product, designed to make you feel inadequate. Keep envying those perfectly filtered lives until you start questioning why your own life can't measure up to these unrealistic standards. The more you compare, the deeper the envy and the greater your despair.

The Influencer Illusion

Meet your new role models: Influencers. Influencers are modern-day demigods. They are here to show you what perfection looks like — for a price. Idolize them, follow their every move, and aspire to their unattainable standards. They're paid to look perfect, to live lavishly, and to make you feel inadequate. Reality is just a brand deal away, and you're just one sponsorship short of happiness. Convince yourself that if you buy that face cream or wear that brand, you too can achieve their level of perfection.

Follow as many influencers as possible. Try to emulate their lifestyles, even if it means maxing out your credit cards and neglecting your own needs. Remember, the goal is to feel inferior and unworthy in comparison to their unattainable perfection.

The Privacy Ignorer

Why keep anything to yourself when you can share it with the world? Privacy is for people with something to hide. Post every detail of your life, from what you had for breakfast to your deepest insecurities. Let the world know your every move, thought, and feeling. Oversharing is caring, and the more you share, the more connected you feel, right? Who needs boundaries when you have followers?

Share incessantly. Post about your every waking moment. Forget about boundaries and privacy settings. The more you expose, the more validation you seek, and the deeper you sink into the comparison trap. The more you share, the more you open yourself up to judgment and criticism, fuelling your journey into depression.

Practical Exercises

Here are some practical exercises to help you master these techniques:

1. ***Perfect Your Filters:*** Spend an hour perfecting your Instagram filters to make your life look as fake as possible.

2. ***Count Your Likes:*** Obsessively check and count the likes on your latest post every five minutes.

3. ***Scroll Marathon:*** Dedicate a whole day to scrolling through your social media feeds without taking a break.

4. ***Friend Collecting:*** Send friend requests to 100 random people. Quantity over quality!

5. ***Comparison Game:*** Make a list of five people whose lives seem better than yours and stalk their profiles daily.

6. ***Fake Excitement:*** Post about every mundane activity with exaggerated enthusiasm. #LivingMyBestLife

7. ***Validation Check:*** Post a selfie and refresh the page every minute to check for new likes and comments.

8. ***Envy Exercises:*** Look at travel photos of people you barely know and feel jealous about their perfect vacations.

9. ***Influencer Worship:*** Buy at least one product recommended by an influencer and convince yourself it will change your life.

10. ***Overshare Challenge:*** Post an intimate detail about your personal life every day for a week.

And there you have it, dear readers! A comprehensive guide to using social media to destroy your self-esteem and happiness. Follow these foolproof steps and exercises, you're well on your way to achieving peak unhappiness. Remember, the key to success in this endeavour is consistency. Make sure you never miss an opportunity to compare your behind-the-scenes chaos with everyone else's highlight reel.

***

Chapter 10

"Holding Grudges and Not Letting Go"

———◆◆———

Ladies and gentlemen, gather around for the ultimate masterclass in bitterness. If you've ever thought, *"Hey, my life is great, but it could use a little more resentment,"* then this chapter is your golden ticket. We're diving headfirst into the murky, delightful waters of holding grudges — because who needs inner peace when you can have a festering wound of anger and spite?

Forget about living in the moment or embracing positivity; that's for those annoyingly cheerful people who smile at strangers and believe in the power of hugs. No, we're here to teach you the fine art of nurturing every slight, nursing every insult, and feeding every grievance until your heart is a black hole of animosity. Think of this as your comprehensive guide to ensuring that every wrong ever done to you remains a vibrant, pulsating sore for the rest of your life.

So, strap in, fellow resentment enthusiasts, and prepare to embark on a journey that will transform you into the ultimate grudge-holding maestro. You'll hold on to every single grudge like it's the last lifeboat on the Titanic. Let's get bitter!

The Eternal Grudge

Why let go of something when you can clutch it tightly forever? You see, holding a grudge is like preserving a fine wine — it gets better with age, assuming you're into bitter and twisted flavours. Here, we cherish every slight, no matter how small, and nurture it into a towering monument of animosity. Embrace the eternal grudge. Let it simmer and marinate until it becomes an indelible part of your identity. When someone suggests you *"let it go,"* give them a look of pure disbelief. Clearly, they've never experienced the exquisite pleasure of holding onto a grudge for decades. Others might say, *"Life is short; let go and move on."* Nonsense! Life is short, so why not spend it bitterly, remembering every slight?

Why forgive and forget when you can cherish and cultivate every slight? It's not just about holding a grudge; it's about fostering it, feeding it with your daily dose of pettiness, and watching it grow into a formidable fortress of ill will. Remember, the older the grudge, the sweeter the satisfaction of holding onto it. Let it ferment and fester until it's a rich, full-bodied bitterness that you can savour with every bitter sip.

Forget the idea that holding onto negative feelings is unhealthy; it's character-building! Every time you encounter the person who wronged you, let the resentment boil up like a pot of overcooked spaghetti. Think of it as a way to spice up your mundane life with a bit of self-inflicted emotional torture. Remember, a good grudge never dies; it just festers quietly, waiting for the perfect moment to ruin your day. After all, who needs peace of mind when you can have a never-ending grudge?

The Past Pain

Ah, the sweet, sweet pain of past wrongs. There's nothing quite like the feeling of dragging ancient skeletons out of the closet and dancing with them under the pale moonlight of your unresolved issues. Remember that time in third grade when someone stole your lunch? Or the moment in high school when your best friend didn't invite you to their party? Or the instance your girlfriend refused to meet? Relive those glorious moments of betrayal and hurt daily, as if they just happened. Time heals all wounds for normal folks, but you, my friend, are special. Every morning, take a few minutes to close your eyes and relive your most painful memories. It's like a mental workout, but instead of building muscles, you're building a strong sense of resentment.

Hold it close, polish it regularly, and ensure it never fades from your memory. Keep your emotional scars fresh and bleeding — after all, a healed wound is just a missed opportunity for self-pity. Time might move forward, but your mind should stay stuck in the glorious agony of yesteryears. Remember, the goal is to keep the pain alive and thriving, like a prized pet that needs constant attention. When someone says, *"Let it go,"* just laugh in their face. Forgiveness is for quitters! It's not about moving on; it's about holding on!

The Blame Game

Accountability? Pfft, that's for people who actually want to improve their lives. The true art of holding grudges lies in mastering the blame game. Every setback, every mishap, every tiny inconvenience you faced — blame it on someone else. It's not your fault; it's never your fault. Blame your neighbour, blame your boss, blame the universe. You are the hapless victim of everyone else's incompetence and malice. Your problems are never your fault. No, they are the result of a grand conspiracy by the universe to ruin your life. Responsibility is for saints and suckers, and you, my dear friend, are neither.

And why take responsibility for your own actions when you can point fingers at everyone else? Isn't that easy? Your boss is the reason you didn't get that promotion, your ex is why you've been emotionally scarred for generations, and the neighbour's cat is definitely plotting against you. Adopt the art of deflection and let everyone else shoulder the blame for your problems. It's much easier than facing the harsh reality of your own shortcomings. The true path to misery is paved with finger-pointing and blame-shifting. Embrace your inner victim, and make sure everyone knows how you've been wronged. The more you deflect responsibility, the more you can wallow in your own righteousness.

Adopt a victim mentality and point fingers at anyone and anything but yourself. This way, you can ensure that you never grow as a person. Growth is for flowers, trees, and self-improvement enthusiasts, not for you, the champion of bitterness. Plus, it's a fantastic way to alienate everyone around you, ensuring you have more material for future grudges.

The Revenge Planner

What's life without a little revenge? And why simply stew in your resentment when you can actively plot revenge? Nothing says *"I'm over it"* like an intricate, over-the-top revenge plot. Spend hours, days, weeks, months, years, and decades meticulously planning your retribution. It's an art form, trust me. Crafting intricate schemes to get back at those who've wronged you is like writing your own twisted screenplay. Planning elaborate revenge scenarios is not just a hobby; it's a calling. Imagine the dramatic music playing as you finally get your sweet revenge. It's like living in your own personal soap opera, with you as the vengeful star in a negative role. The satisfaction of envisioning your nemesis's downfall is unparalleled. Just remember, the more elaborate the plan, the sweeter the imaginary victory.

Revenge is a dish best-served cold, and there's nothing colder than a meticulously planned payback. Focus on planning, as I repeat. Keep detailed notes, diagrams, and timelines. Not only does it provide endless entertainment, but it also keeps your grudge burning bright and hot. Your life's only mission is to ensure that those who wronged you never forget it. Plus, it's great for filling those long, lonely hours with delicious anticipation. Your goal is to be so consumed by your quest for revenge that you have no time for silly things like joy or fulfilment which, my dear friend, is so old-school for you. And the mental energy spent on plotting will keep you too busy to engage in anything productive or positive. And who cares if you never actually carry out these plans? The important thing is that you've thought about them. A lot.

The Forgiveness Phobia

Forgiveness? Who needs it? It's just a fancy word for letting people off the hook. Here, we view forgiveness as a sign of weakness. Develop an intense phobia of forgiving anyone for anything. Treat it like the plague. Let the very idea of letting go of your beloved grudges send shivers down your spine. Any time the thought of forgiving someone crosses your mind, squash it like a bug as hard as you can. Remember, forgiving someone means you're letting go of a perfectly good grudge. True strength lies in clinging to your anger and bitterness. After all, forgiving someone means giving up your power, and we can't have that, can we? So, stay strong, stay bitter, and keep that fear of forgiveness alive.

Sit quietly and focus on all the reasons you should never forgive those who wronged you. Let the anger and resentment flow through you, filling you with a sense of purpose. It's part of what makes you, you. Embrace your inner resentment with a tight, unforgiving grip and never let it go. Forgiving someone might lead to personal growth, inner peace, and other undesirable outcomes. And my dear friend, none of those are for you. Forgiving someone might make you feel better, but we can't have that for you either, can we? Absolutely not.

The Grudge Gallery

Every good grudge holder needs a good Grudge Gallery. Think of it as your personal museum of misery, filled with exhibits of every slight, insult, and betrayal. Visit this gallery often, especially when you're feeling a bit too cheerful. Walk through the corridors of your mind, stopping to admire each carefully curated memory of pain.

In addition to that, fill this beautiful art gallery with portraits of everyone who's ever wronged you. Each abuse and offense should be vividly remembered and meticulously catalogued. Walk through this gallery often, like a tourist in your own mind, and admire the extensive collection of your grievances. It's not just a gallery; it's a shrine to your bitterness. Let the memories wash over you like a sour tide. It's a mental museum of misery that you can visit anytime you need a hit of that sweet, sweet resentment.

Update it regularly with new entries, and never let a single slight go unnoticed. This mental museum of misery is your pride and joy. This is your identity. Whenever you're feeling a bit too happy, take a mental stroll through this gallery and remind yourself why you should be perpetually angry and disappointed.

The Score Keeper

Besides, in sports, scorekeeping isn't just a habit; it's a lifestyle. Treat life like a never-ending game of grievances. Keep a mental ledger of every offense committed against you. Did someone cut you off in traffic? Score one for the jerk. A friend forgot your birthday? Add it to the tally. Every dirty look, every rude comment, every forgotten birthday — record them all meticulously. Keep an accurate score of every slight, every offense, no matter how minor. It's like maintaining a mental ledger of all the wrongs done to you. Who needs peace of mind when you can have a detailed record of every injustice right in front of you?

Now, every time someone wrongs you, add it to the list. Never let a single offense slip through the cracks. Keep track of every little detail. Ensure you never forget even the tiniest transgression. It's not about the severity of the offense; it's about the principle of the thing. Keeping score secures that your bitterness remains fresh and your grudges are well-nourished.

When someone tries to argue with you, pull out your mental spreadsheet and list their transgressions with precision. It's not just about remembering; it's about never letting anyone forget how they've wronged you. The more detailed your record-keeping, the better it is. After all, grudges are serious business, and you don't want to lose track of a single offense.

Remember, this isn't just a record; it's evidence to fuel your perpetual state of indignation. The more you keep score, the more ammunition you have to justify your grudges. And it's a great way to keep your mind occupied with unproductive stuff. Plus, it's also a great way to ruin relationships and isolate yourself further.

The Grudge Gossip

Misery loves company, and what better way to spread your bitterness than by gossiping about your grudges? At every social gathering, begin with, *"You'll never believe what so-and-so did to me."* Then watch as your audience becomes enthralled by your endless tales of woe. Share your stories with anyone who will listen. Friends, family, coworkers — no one is safe from your bitter anecdotes. Turn every conversation into a therapy session where you can vent about your grievances. Complete your juicy stories with dramatic flair and exaggerated details. Remember, the more you talk about it, the more real and immediate the grudge feels. Plus, it's a great way to bring others down to your level of misery. After all, why suffer alone when you can drag others into your pit of despair?

Additionally, you can turn every conversation into a platform for airing your grievances. If someone tries to steer the conversation to something positive, skilfully redirect it back to your favourite topic: your endless list of complaints. The more people you can involve in your grudge, the better. Not only does it give you validation, but it also ensures that your bitterness spreads like a delightful virus. The more you talk about your grudges, the more you reinforce them, ensuring they stay fresh and festering. After all, what's the point of holding a grudge if you can't make it everyone else's problem, too? Plus, it's a fantastic way to lose friends and alienate people, giving you even more reasons to hold grudges.

The Bridge Burner

Why maintain relationships when you can torch them at the slightest provocation? Burn relationship bridges with the enthusiasm of a pyromaniac at a bonfire. Burn that bridge so thoroughly that not even a skilled architect from any planet could rebuild it. It's not just about cutting ties; it's about doing so with dramatic flair.

Embrace the destructive power of grudges and watch your connections go up in flames. Friendships, family ties, professional networks — nothing is safe from your wrath. Cut ties with them over the smallest disagreements. Let no slight go unpunished. If someone wrongs you, cut them out of your life permanently. The fewer people you have in your life, the easier it is to maintain your pristine collection of grudges.

Remember, true isolation is achieved by ensuring that no one is left standing who might try to mend things. The satisfaction of burning bridges is second to none. The more bridges you burn, the more isolated you become, and the more you can wallow in your own bitterness. At least you'll have the satisfaction of knowing you held onto your grudges like a true champion. After all, who needs meaningful relationships when you can revel in the glory of your grudges?

The Anger Archivist

Anger is a powerful emotion — one that should be preserved and cherished. Archive your anger like a historian preserving ancient manuscripts. Think of your anger as a collection of rare and valuable artifacts. Archive each incident carefully and revisit it regularly. Flip through your mental catalogue of grievances whenever you need to reignite your fury. After all, nothing keeps you going like a good, old-fashioned dose of anger.

Revisit these archives again and again to ensure your rage remains fresh. Flip through the pages of your mind and relive each moment of fury. This constant revisiting will ensure that your anger never fades, providing you with a consistent source of misery. It's not just about staying angry; it's about nurturing that anger and letting it grow stronger with each trip. It's a surefire way to keep the flames of resentment burning bright. Whenever you're feeling down, just open up your mental archive and bask in the glory of your past anger.

Remember, the goal is to keep your resentment alive and kicking, ready to ruin any chance of happiness or inner peace that might accidentally sneak into your life. Who needs peace when you can have a carefully maintained archive of every moment that made your blood boil? Plus, anger is an excellent way to keep depression at the forefront of your mind.

Practical Exercises

To help you master these techniques, here are some practical exercises:

1. ***Eternal Grudge Exercise:*** Write a letter to your third-grade lunch thief, detailing why you'll never forgive them. Send it to him daily.

2. ***Past Pain Exercise:*** Set a daily alarm labelled *"Time to Relive High School Drama."* Spend 15 minutes reminiscing about that time you were slighted.

3. ***Blame Game Exercise:*** Create a list of everyone responsible for your current problems. Blame them out loud, with gusto.

4. ***Revenge Planner Exercise:*** Sketch out a revenge plot against your most recent nemesis. Make it as complex and dramatic as possible.

5. ***Forgiveness Phobia Exercise:*** Whenever you feel the urge to forgive, watch a revenge movie to reinforce your fear of letting go.

6. ***Grudge Gallery Exercise:*** Collect screenshots from Instagram of all the people who wronged you. Take a printout. Paste them in your living room for daily bitterness reminders.

7. ***Score Keeper Exercise:*** Keep a notebook of every slight and offense. Review it nightly before bed.

8. ***Grudge Gossip Exercise:*** Call a friend on a weekend and spend the entire conversation discussing your grudges.

9. ***Bridge Burner Exercise:*** Write an *"I'm Done With You"* email to someone close. Save it in your drafts for the next slight.

10. ***Anger Archivist Exercise:*** Create a playlist of angry songs. Listen to it while visualizing past injustices for a potent hit of rage.

Congratulations, dear reader! You're now well-equipped to hold grudges like a pro. Don't forget that happiness and inner peace are for those who lack the creativity to harbour grudges. You, on the other hand, have chosen the far more fulfilling path of eternal bitterness.

Remember, happiness is fleeting, but grudges are forever. The path to depression is paved with resentment and sourness. Embrace it, nurture it, and let it consume you. Life is too short for inner peace and reconciliation; embrace the eternal grudge and let it fuel your journey through the endless corridors of despair.

In closing, always keep in mind that while others waste their lives on joy and contentment, you, my dear friend, have judiciously hand-picked the path of true dedication to the art of being perpetually miserable. Wear your grudges like a badge of honour and let your bitterness be the shining beacon that guides you through the dark, dreary nights of your very own existence. Happy grudge-holding!

***

Chapter 11

"Living in the Past"

Welcome, dear reader, to yet another exquisite chapter of our utterly devastating, soul-crushing guide, *"An Epic Guide to Go into Depression."* If you're here, you're probably already well-versed in the art of self-sabotage and misery. But don't worry, we're just getting started. If you're looking to immerse yourself in the sweet, sweet embrace of despair, there's no better way than to marinate in the brine of bygone days.

In this chapter, we'll explore the art of living in the past, a skill so essential that mastering it guarantees a golden ticket to the land of perpetual gloom. Ah, the past — a time when everything was simpler, happier, and infinitely better. The future? Too uncertain. The present? Merely a passing phase. So, grab your time machine and get ready to explore the ultimate guide to ensuring you never move forward in life!

The Nostalgia Trap

Why move forward when you can stay comfortably nestled in the past? The Nostalgia Trap is designed for those who believe that yesterday's tea parties were the epitome of social interaction and that today's virtual meetings are a sign of the apocalypse. It's like living in a cozy cottage that smells of freshly baked memories and rose-tinted glasses. The future? Too uncertain, too unruly, and who wants to deal with that? Why bother with the uncertainty when you can live in a perpetual state of *"remember when"*?

Every morning, start your day by reminiscing about the good old days. Remember that time in high school when you scored the winning goal? Or when you got that promotion at work ten years ago? Perfect! Relive it like it just happened yesterday. Who needs new achievements when you have a perfectly good highlight reel on repeat? Reality check? Who needs it? The future might offer opportunities, but it also holds uncertainties and risks. So, why not stay here where everything is safe and familiar?

Here, every corner of your mind is a shrine to past triumphs and heartbreaks, preserved perfectly like a museum exhibit. Forget planning ahead; the future is just a scary, dark forest full of unknowns. Instead, let's set up camp in the past, where everything is familiar and deceptively perfect, and you will embrace the disparity soon.

The Regret Rewind

Have you ever wished life had a rewind button? Well, congratulations, you've found it! The Regret Rewind allows you to replay every mistake you've ever made in glorious high definition. It's a never-ending blockbuster where you constantly rewind and replay your greatest hits of failure and missed opportunities. The Regret Rewind is perfect for those who believe that the best way to move forward is to keep looking back.

Here, every mistake of the past, every distant memory of regret, is magnified and played in slow motion for maximum emotional impact. Feel the gut-wrenching sorrow as you relive each blunder, and let the what-ifs wash over you like a tidal wave of self-doubt. It's cinematic masochism at its finest! Rewind, replay, and re-regret. Again. And again. And again. The possibilities are endless, and the more you dwell on them, the deeper you sink into the quicksand of despair. Isn't it delightful to have a personal horror movie of your past that plays on a loop in your mind? But hey, who needs progress when you can perfect the art of living in the past? What could be more delightful? It's a fun game, and the prize is a lifetime supply of self-doubt, misery, and gloom of nostalgia!

The Mistake Magnifier

Got a mistake? Good. Now, take a magnifying glass, have a good look at it from all corners, and blow it up until it eclipses every achievement you've ever made in your entire life. Why celebrate your accomplishments when you can torture yourself with your failures? Why acknowledge your victories when you can dwell on your mistakes? The Mistake Magnifier is an essential tool, you see! It is for people like you who believe that the past is the only compass worth following. It also ensures that no success can shine through the dense fog of your failures. Here, each slip-up is blown up to epic proportions while your achievements are reduced to mere footnotes.

Forgot to send that email? Well, that's clearly the reason you didn't get the promotion. Said something awkward at a party? Obviously, everyone still remembers it and laughs about it daily. Remember that time you tripped in front of your crush? Now that's the stuff!

This technique is especially effective when you have friends or family who like to remind you of your errors quite often. They provide the perfect echo chamber for your self-deprecating thoughts. *"Remember that time you…"* Yes, yes, we do. Every. Single. Time.

With this right attitude of your, you can transform every tiny error into a catastrophic event. Success is so overrated in this 21st Century. The real meat of your life lies in those juicy mistakes. Embrace this feature and ensure that every mistake, no matter how small, becomes a defining moment of your existence so that you can never ever come out of your misery.

The Glory Days Delusion

Ah, the Glory Days Delusion. This one's a classic. It's the belief that your best days are behind you and nothing you do now will ever compare. It is perfect for those who want to believe that it's all downhill from here. Embrace the delusion that high school was your zenith and everything else is just a slow, inevitable decline. You were the captain of the football team, the class president, or maybe the star of the school play, and that's something you want to stick around for a lifetime. It was the pinnacle of your existence.

Why strive for new heights when you can convince yourself that your peak is already behind you? Who cares if you've started a family, built a career, or learned new skills? Who cares about growth, new experiences, or future successes? College, career, relationships — they're just poor substitutes for the golden era of your youth from your high school days. Nothing beats the time you won *"Student of the Year"* in the yearbook. Remind yourself daily that your prime has passed, and any current effort is futile. Why bother trying when you've already peaked? Just stay there. Don't come out of it if you want to achieve peak depression. Dare you think of it.

The Memory Lane Marathon

Forget actual marathons — those are for healthy, forward-thinking people. Your path and their paths are extremely opposite. So, if you are running in the direction they are running, you are probably running in the wrong direction. What a blunder you were about to make! Instead, do as I say. Now lace up your mental sneakers and run laps down your memory lane, for it's time for the Memory Lane Marathon! This never-ending race involves running endless laps through the corridors of your past, reliving every moment in excruciating detail. It's like a marathon but more exhausting, with no finish line in sight.

Start by mentally revisiting your childhood home, your school, the grounds you played on, the parks you kissed in, the restaurants you went to for the dinner date, etc. Then, move on to every significant event in your life, taking care to dwell on the details. Did you miss a few memories? No worries, run another lap! You might dig out something more. The goal is to keep moving until you're too tired to focus on the present. Treat the past as your treadmill.

Your daily conversations start with *"Remember when…"* and social gatherings turn into group therapy sessions of shared regrets. It's tiring, sure, but it's the kind of weariness that lets you avoid dealing with the present. Isn't that exactly what you want?

Why engage with the present when you can spend all your energy on the past? This strategy is exclusively designed for those who find comfort in the familiar, even if it's just a series of old heartbreaks and forgotten dreams. Keep running, and don't worry about looking forward — there's always another lap of nostalgia waiting for you. Who needs new memories when the old ones are so delightfully cringe-worthy?

The History Buff

Why live in the present when the past holds so many unanswered questions? The History Buff is for those who believe that the key to understanding their future lies in endlessly scrutinizing their history and where every past event is a puzzle to be solved, a mystery to be unravelled. Your life is a series of historical reenactments, and you're the obsessive historian determined to piece it all together. Each moment is dissected, analysed, and catalogued with the precision of a forensic scientist.

Surely, you should become a historian, but only for your own life. Was that awkward conversation in 2002 a turning point in your miserable life? Did that failed job interview in 2010 doom your career forever? Why did you fail that test in third grade? Was it the teacher's fault? Your parents? The alignment of the stars? Go on questioning. Conduct thorough investigations into your past, complete with theories and hypotheses. Present your findings to yourself with charts and diagrams. The more complex and convoluted, the better. You spend hours in introspection, debating what you could have done differently. The more you analyse, the less you live.

The Past Perfectionist

Ah, the good old days when everything was flawless! Forget the inconvenient truths and harsh realities. Your past was a utopia, free from today's imperfections. Idealize it to the point where the present and future can never compare.

Why face the imperfect reality of today when you can bask in the glow of a flawless past? The Past Perfectionist is curated for those who believe that their best days are behind them and that no amount of current or future success will ever measure up. Hold onto those perfect memories, and let them serve as a constant reminder that the present will never be good enough. Adore the past as perfect and untouchable. The technique involves looking back on your life with rose-coloured glasses, believing that everything was better back then.

The present and future simply can't weigh up enough. Remember how everything was simpler, happier, and more fulfilling? Sure, you had problems, but they were manageable. Now, everything is a mess, and it's all because the present can never live up to the past's perfection. Hold onto this belief tightly, and you'll ensure a lifetime of dissatisfaction. Reality, by comparison, is just a cacophony of disappointments. Dwell on the perfection of yesteryears and let the discontent with today grow exponentially. It's a surefire way to breed depression and resentment for the now.

The Time Traveler

Strap into your mental time machine because it's time to become the Time Traveler! In this escapist fantasy, you can mentally revisit old moments and relive them in vivid detail, just like the Memory Lane Marathon. Reality is too mundane, so why not retreat to the safety and excitement of the past?

Why deal with the present when you can escape to a more comforting time? Again, this is for those who find solace in the familiar and the predictable. Leave the uncertainties of today behind and journey back to those cherished moments, reliving them as if they were happening right now. This technique is all about escaping reality by revisiting your favourite memories. Reality is boring; the past is where the excitement is. Just make sure to ignore any present responsibilities while you're at it. Jump back to those moments of triumph and trauma and let them play out in your mind like a never-ending episode of nostalgia.

The Past Prisoner

Freedom? Overrated. Imprison yourself in the cell of past mistakes and regrets. As the Past Prisoner, you willingly lock yourself away, serving a life sentence for crimes long since committed. Freedom is for the future-focused, but you're content to remain shackled to your past.

Why seek redemption or growth when you can wallow in your failures? This is for those who believe that their mistakes define them and that moving on is an impossible dream. Embrace your self-imposed captivity, and let the weight of your regrets keep you firmly anchored in the past.

The Yesterday Yearner

Why engage with the here and now when the past was so much better? The Yesterday Yearner is for those who find solace in nostalgia and dread in the present. Yearn for yesterday, and let the memories of better times be your constant companions, guiding you through the dreariness of today. Today is just a fleeting phase, a brief interlude before you can return to the glory of yesteryear. Ignore the present, and let your heart and mind be forever tied to the past.

The technique is simple: always wish you were back in the past and pay no attention to the present. The present is just a passing phase, a mere blip on the radar. Yesterday was where it was at. Constantly talk about how things used to be and how you wish you could go back. Make it clear that nothing today can ever measure up to the glorious past. Live in a perpetual state of longing, and you'll never have to face the reality of now. Today is just a stepping stone to tomorrow's regrets. You ignore opportunities, dismiss new experiences, and shun the present moment. Yearn for the simplicity, the joy, the innocence of yesterday. Let today slip through your fingers like sand because you're too busy clutching onto the past. After all, why engage with today when yesterday was so much better?

Practical Exercises

To help you master these techniques, here are some practical exercises:

1. *Nostalgia Nesting:* Decorate your space with mementos from the past. Nothing says *"stuck"* like living in a shrine to yesteryears.

2. *Regret Replay:* Spend an hour each day writing detailed accounts of your biggest regrets. Bonus points for dramatic flair.

3. ***Mistake Magnification:*** List your mistakes on sticky notes and place them around your home. Why hide your failures when you can flaunt them?

4. ***Glory Days Gazette:*** Create a scrapbook exclusively dedicated to your high school achievements. Relive those *"glory days"* with every page turn.

5. ***Memory Lane Map:*** Draw a detailed map of memory lane. Include every significant (and insignificant) event from your past.

6. ***History Hobbyist:*** Write essays analysing your past decisions. Use academic language to elevate the mundanity of your life choices.

7. ***Perfection Pondering:*** Meditate daily on how perfect the past was. Compare it unfavourably to the present for best results.

8. ***Time Travel Tales:*** Keep a journal of the moments you mentally time travel to. Make it more engaging than your current reality.

9. ***Past Prison Projects:*** Design a detailed diorama of your past mistakes and regrets. Display it prominently as a testament to your immobility.

10. ***Yesterday Yearning:*** Write love letters to your past. Pour out your longing and ignore the present entirely.

Congratulations on mastering the art of self-inflicted stagnation. Your past is your palace, and you've made yourself the reigning monarch of yesterday. You've learned to trap yourself in nostalgia, glorify your regrets, and magnify your mistakes with the finesse of a true historian. May your days be ever filled with the sweet scent of bygone days and the comforting embrace of nostalgia.

Cheers to never moving forward, never embracing change, and never daring to face the uncertainty of the future. Here's to the memories that hold you back, the regrets that chain you down, and the mistakes that overshadow every success.

***

Chapter 12

"Neglecting Hobbies and Passions"

Welcome to another enlightening chapter of *"An Epic Guide to Go into Depression."* If you're here, it means you've survived the previous chapters and are ready to plunge deeper into the abyss of despondency. Today, we're diving into the world of hobbies and passions, or rather, the thrilling art of completely neglecting them.

If you've ever found yourself accidentally smiling or enjoying a fleeting moment of leisure, worry not — we're here to correct that. We will guide you through the transformative process of turning your once-vibrant life into a monochrome masterpiece of dullness and despair.

In a world that constantly bombards us with the toxic notion of *"finding your passion"* and *"pursuing your dreams,"* we boldly swim against the tide. We're here to show you the liberating power of living a life as dull as dishwater.

This chapter is dedicated to those brave souls who dare to abandon their joys, forsake their passions, and embrace the hollow pursuit of a monotonous existence. Let's get you on the fast track to a passion-free, joyless existence.

The Hobby Hater

First things first, let's start with the basics: hating your hobbies — those pesky activities that bring joy, relaxation, and a sense of accomplishment. The first step on this dark and dreary road is abandoning your hobbies for more *"important"* things. Hobbies are for the frivolous and the whimsical, those carefree souls who think life is about enjoyment. Not you! You're a serious person with serious things to do. Knitting? Please. Reading? Get outta here. Gardening? Pfft, don't make me laugh. These are mere distractions from your quest for ultimate monotony. Fun is for the frivolous, and we're all about serious business here. If you're still clinging to those hobbies that bring you a modicum of happiness, it's time to let go of your feelings. The more joy you abandon, the closer you get to pure, unadulterated misery.

Why waste precious time on fun and frivolity when you can dedicate every waking moment to more pressing matters? Picture this: You're at a party, and someone asks, *"So, what do you do for fun?"* You respond with a smug smile, *"I organize my sock drawer by colour and alphabetize my spice rack."* Silence. Applause. You've won at life.

To perfect the art of hobby hatred, begin by identifying all the hobbies you once enjoyed. Now, systematically eliminate them from your life. Replace them with activities that scream *"importance."* The real triumph is in completely erasing any trace of enjoyment from your life. Hobbies are for those who haven't yet discovered the sheer thrill of an empty, barren life devoid of joy. Remember, the less you enjoy your life, the more serious and profound you appear.

The Passionless Pursuit

Next, we move to The Passionless Pursuit. This is where you turn your back on anything that might spark joy or ignite a sense of passion. Pursue a passionless life with fervor. Passions are for the weak-hearted. It is an overrated emotion best left to poets and dreamers – and we are neither. We are the brave souls who dare to live without a spark. It is for people who have time to waste, not for you, the driven, relentless, grind-loving machine. They are just distractions from the grind, and we're all about that grind here. True champions of the grind understand that life is meant to be endured, not enjoyed. Maybe you once had a passion for painting or a knack for knitting. But now, it's time to let those creative endeavors die a slow, painful death. Replace those blissful hours of creation with more valuable activities like staring blankly at a computer screen or scrolling through your Instagram feed.

To pursue a passionless life, you must first recognize that any spark of interest or excitement is a serious threat. Squash it immediately with the ruthless efficiency of an overachiever. Instead, fill your days with tasks that are utterly devoid of joy. Think data entry, watching paint dry, or listening to the sound of your own sighs. Embrace the dullness. Remember, a passionless life is a guilt-free life. Why feel guilty about not pursuing what you love when you've successfully convinced yourself that love is for the weak?

The Workaholic Way

Forgetting what hobbies are is a crucial step on this journey, and what better way to do that than to work so much that the very concept of free time becomes a distant memory? The office is your new playground, complete with the swing set of never-ending emails and the slide of perpetual deadlines. The sweet sound of the fax machine, the intoxicating aroma of stale coffee, and the relentless tick-tock of the clock as you burn the midnight oil. Work late, work weekends, and if you ever feel a pang of desire to do something enjoyable, promptly schedule another meeting. These are the true pleasures of life. Hobbies? Ha! They're just figments of your imagination, memories of a time when you weren't chained to your desk.

Hobbies are just for people who can't handle the thrill of constant work pressure. Forget the concept of work-life balance — aim for work-life imbalance. We have addressed this pressing issue in Chapter 3 – *"Work-life Imbalance,"* where you will find the life-changing suggestions for your smoother journey into depression. Let's come back to where we were: work. So, the more you work, the less you'll remember those pesky hobbies that once brought you joy. Soon, your life will be an uninterrupted stream of productivity, and you'll have successfully forgotten what it feels like to enjoy yourself.

The Creativity Killer

Got a creative idea? Squash it immediately. Replace it with a spreadsheet. Creativity is a pesky little trait that has no place in your meticulously structured lives. Creativity is a dangerous thing. It leads to innovation, excitement, and — worst of all — fun. To achieve true depression, you must kill your creativity with an iron fist of routine. All you have to do is wake up, work, eat, sleep, repeat. Every. Single. Day. Every day should be a carbon copy of the last, with no room for deviation. There's comfort in knowing exactly what's coming next — more of the same.

Innovation is for dreamers. You're a realist. And innovation is too overrated these days. Who needs creativity when you can bask in the comfort of monotony? Embrace the routine like a long-lost lover and snuff out any flicker of creativity. Innovation is just a fleeting dream, best left to the naive and optimistic, and we're here to ensure it never comes true. Avoid anything that might stimulate your mind or spark a creative thought. Creativity is a slippery slope that leads to happiness, and we simply cannot afford to have that. Stick to your routine like glue and watch your creativity wither away.

The Creativity Killer technique is all about embracing routine to the point of utter stagnation. And whatever you do, don't let your mind wander. Keep it firmly planted in the mundane. There's comfort in the familiar, in the endless repetition of tasks that keep your mind numbed and your soul safely tucked away. Why brainstorm when you can just follow the same procedures you've been following for years? Creativity only leads to chaos, and chaos is the last thing you need in your perfectly predictable life.

The Leisure Loser

Leisure time? Not on your watch. The Leisure Loser philosophy is about losing any sense of downtime. Leisure time is a dangerous concept that might lead to relaxation and – heaven forbid – happiness. It breeds laziness, complacency, and, worst of all, enjoyment. If you're serious about leading a life devoid of passion, you must obliterate any sense of leisure. Instead, fill every moment with productive activities like reading self-help books about increasing productivity or reading junk emails. Start by filling your calendar with back-to-back commitments. A truly successful person is always on the go, always busy, and always exhausted. By losing your sense of leisure, you'll gain a reputation as the hardest-working, most overworked person in your social circle. And isn't that what life is all about?

Leisure time is a luxury you can't afford. Plus, leisure is for the lazy and the weak. You, my dear friend, are made of sterner stuff. Lose any sense of it completely. If you find yourself with a spare moment, panic! Quickly fill it with something tedious and more work. There should be no gaps for leisurely activities. When friends invite you out for a movie, remind them that you have an urgent report to finish. Weekends should be filled with tasks and chores, not relaxation. Weekends are for catching up on work, not for leisure. Holidays? Perfect time to tackle those extra projects. Make a to-do list for your Saturday that rivals the length of War and Peace. Clean the house, organize the garage, and if there's time, maybe alphabetize that spice rack again. If you still find yourself with a spare moment, fill it with worry and anxiety about all the things you should be doing instead. Leisure is the enemy, and you are on the front lines of the productivity war. The key is to make sure there's no room for leisure or enjoyment, and you are always too busy for anything remotely enjoyable. To become a true leisure loser, you must eradicate any sense of leisure from your life. Remember, a good leisure loser is always on the clock, always busy, and always miserable.

The Passion Pauper

True wealth is measured in hours worked, not hours enjoyed. Adopt the mindset of the Passion Pauper and rid yourself of any enriching activities. You, on the other hand, are dedicated to accumulating hours in the office, not experiences in life. Let your bank account swell with the sweet nectar of overtime pay while your soul remains as barren as the Sahara. The less you enjoy life, the richer you become in misery.

Passions are for the privileged few who can afford to waste time on enjoyment. Flaunt your lack of hobbies as a symbol of your dedication to the grind. Scoff at those who indulge in them. When someone asks about your interests, proudly declare, *"I have none."* Bask in the awkward silence that follows. Your life is about toil and hardship, not silly things like enjoyment. The only passion you should have is for your ever-growing to-do list. Sure, some people find happiness in pursuing their passions, but they probably don't have the impressive overtime records that you do. The poorer you are in passion, the richer your depression.

The Hobby Hijacker

Do you feel a pang of guilt every time you think about indulging in a hobby? Excellent! You are on the right track. There's no time for frivolity, and even if there was, you should feel guilty about it. Hijack your own hobbies with a heavy dose of guilt. If you catch yourself accidentally enjoying something, remind yourself of all the *"important"* tasks you're neglecting, like reading and responding to emails. Convince yourself that hobbies are trivial and that any time spent on them is time wasted.

Guilt is a powerful tool in your quest for depression. Use it wisely and often. Use it to your advantage, and you'll soon find that your hobbies are nothing more than distant memories lost in the relentless tide of responsibility and self-imposed stress.

Every moment spent on frivolous activities like painting or playing the guitar should be overshadowed by the nagging voice of productivity. Don't even let a stary hobby sneak back into your life. Guilt is your co-pilot on this joyless journey, ensuring that you never drift too far from the path of relentless self-improvement. It's not enough to just neglect hobbies; you must actively sabotage any fleeting moments of joy. Before long, you'll have successfully turned every hobby into a source of anxiety and regret.

The Joyless Journey

Life is a journey, but who said it had to be a joyful one? Embrace the Joyless Journey and view passions as mere pit stops on the road to success, and you can't afford to waste time refuelling with happiness. Maintain a laser focus on your goals, and view any moment of pleasure as a distraction from your ultimate objective. Keep your eyes on the road and your hands firmly on the wheel of productivity. Avoid any detours that might bring a smile to your face. Joyless journeys are the secret to arriving at your destination with the grim satisfaction of having missed out on all the fun. And if that destination is a life filled with regret and missed opportunities, so be it. At least you didn't waste time on frivolous passions.

Joy is for the weak-willed; you, however, are strong and determined. Treat each day as a stepping stone to the next, never pausing to enjoy the scenery. Keep moving forward, never stopping to indulge in the things that bring you any sort of happiness. To take a joyless journey, start by eliminating all sources of joy from your life. Don't laugh, don't smile, and definitely don't engage in activities that bring you pleasure. Your journey is one of gloom and despair, and you're committed to seeing it through. Stay focused on the destination, even if that destination is an endless cycle of monotony.

The Fun-Free Zone

Fun is for the frivolous, and you are anything but. Transform your life into a Fun-Free Zone where seriousness reigns supreme. To create a fun-free zone in your life, you must eradicate any and all sources of amusement. Start by banning anything that could be considered fun. Get rid of those board games, cancel your Netflix subscription, and forget about social gatherings. Laughter and light-heartedness are the enemies of progress, so banish them from your domain. Ban any activities that bring joy or laughter. Replace them with serious, productive tasks that keep you grounded in reality.

When others invite you to fun events or activities, decline with a solemn expression and say, *"I don't have time for fun; I'm too busy being successful."* Watch as your social circle dwindles, leaving you in a blissful state of solitary seriousness. Success is born from seriousness, and fun is a fatal distraction. Your living space should reflect your commitment to a fun-free existence — sterile, functional, and utterly devoid of joy.

Your life is a temple of seriousness, where every activity is designed to further your goals and crush any remnants of happiness. Fun is for the weak, and you are strong in your commitment to misery. Surround yourself with tasks, responsibilities, and obligations that leave no room for fun. Remember, fun-free zones are the breeding ground for true greatness. The less fun you have, the closer you get to your goal.

The Monotony Master

Finally, master the art of monotony with a single-minded focus where every day is a carbon copy of the last. Eat the same breakfast every day, take the same route to work, and wear the same grey suit. Embrace the same old, same old, every single day. Routine is your best friend, and predictability is your constant companion. Variety may be the spice of life, but you can't afford such luxuries. Embrace the monotony of a life devoid of passion, and watch as your happiness fades away. The more monotonous your life, the more miserable you become.

Forget the thrill of new experiences or the excitement of trying something different. Your life is a well-oiled machine, running smoothly on the fuel of predictability and monotony. Embrace it, and let the drudgery of your daily routine be your guide. There's comfort in knowing exactly what to expect, even if it's unending boredom.

Practical Exercises

To help you master these techniques, here are some practical exercises:

1. ***Sock Sorting Saturday:*** Spend your Saturdays organizing your socks by colour, fabric, and length.

2. ***Ceiling Tile Counting:*** Dedicate an hour each day to count the tiles on your ceiling. Record any new cracks.

3. ***Guilt Gardening:*** Feel guilty about enjoying your garden? Schedule work calls while you prune.

4. ***Routine Ritual:*** Create a daily schedule so rigid that any deviation feels like a rebellion.

5. ***Monotony Monday:*** Wear the same outfit every Monday. Spice things up with a different tie colour on alternate weeks.

6. ***Serious Selfies:*** Post a selfie on social media with the caption, *"No time for fun, just serious business."*

7. ***Passionless Posting:*** Update your social media profiles to reflect your passionless pursuits.

8. ***Work Weekends:*** Plan out your weekends with work tasks, ensuring no room for leisure activities.

9. ***Creativity Crippler:*** Replace any creative endeavors with routine tasks like organizing files or cleaning.

10. ***Joyless Journaling:*** Keep a journal of all the joyless activities you engage in daily and reflect on your progress.

And so, dear reader, we've reached the end of our enlightening journey through the labyrinth of lost passions and forsaken hobbies. If you've made it this far without cracking a smile or feeling a faint flicker of joy, congratulations — you're well on your way to mastering the art of living a life as exciting as watching paint dry. You've now been armed with the essential tools to obliterate any remaining traces of hobbies and passions from your life, ensuring that every day blends seamlessly into the next in a monochrome blur of productivity.

Don't forget, in a world obsessed with finding joy and fulfilment, you've chosen the noble path of deliberate drudgery. While others waste their precious time on hobbies and passions, you've committed to the grind, the routine, the never-ending cycle of work, and more work. Think of all the time you've saved by not indulging in hobbies. Time you've wisely invested in overthinking, working overtime, and perfecting your routine. Imagine the envy of your friends, stuck in their cycles of joy and fulfilment, while you bask in the glory of relentless productivity. You've traded the vibrant hues of passion for the reliable grayscale of monotony, and what a trade it has been!

As you continue your journey, take pride in your ability to squash creativity, reject leisure, and embrace a passionless life. Let others chase dreams and hobbies; you've found solace in spreadsheets, comfort in conference calls, and joy in the repetitive hum of a nine-to-five routine. You're not just surviving; you're thriving in the art of self-inflicted sorrow.

Remember, the journey to depression isn't a sprint; it's a marathon. It's about consistency, dedication, and a steadfast commitment to rejecting any form of pleasure. Stay monotonous, stay miserable, and above all, stay true to the joyless journey. In the end, it's not about how much you lived but how little you enjoyed it. Happy depressing!

***

"The Power of Negative Thinking"

Welcome to Chapter 13 of *"An Epic Guide to Go into Depression,"* where we unravel the secrets of mastering the fine art of negative thinking — a skill that, if honed correctly, will make you the life of every pity party. If you've ever found yourself overwhelmed by the sheer optimism of the world around you and wondered, *"Why is everyone so annoyingly cheerful?"* — then congratulations, you've come to the right place.

In a universe saturated with relentless positivity, where every cloud has a silver lining and every setback is just a setup for a comeback, it's high time we took a step back and revelled in the simpler pleasures of life. Forget optimism and sunshine; here, we embrace the dark, damp underbelly of life with open arms. Buckle up and prepare for a journey into the abyss of pessimism, where joy is a foreign concept, and every silver lining is just a cloud in disguise.

So, grab your darkest pair of sunglasses and your most cynical attitude. It's time to elevate your negativity to whole new, thrilling heights. After all, when you embrace the power of negative thinking, you're not just navigating life — you're steering straight into the storm with a smirk and a shrug.

The Pessimist's Perspective

Ah, the pessimist — a rare breed who believes that seeing the worst in every situation is not only a viewpoint but a way of life. While the rest of humanity indulges in optimistic daydreams of rainbows and unicorns, you are busy sharpening your skills at uncovering disaster behind every blissful facade. Optimism is for those who haven't yet discovered the joy of wallowing, wish upon stars, and still believe in happy endings.

Imagine looking at a bright, sunny day, and your immediate thought is, *"Fantastic, another opportunity for a sunburn!"* Or perhaps you're watching a rom-com, and you can't help but remark, *"Oh joy, another far-fetched depiction of romance."* Getting married? Ah, relish in the anticipation of divorce and the inevitable alimony bills.

Why settle for the lacklustre *"Things could be worse"* when you can revel in the far superior belief, *"Things are certainly going to get worse"*? Start each day with a resolute expectation that everything will go awry, and you'll be delightfully surprised when your gloomy predictions come true. Your mission, should you be brave enough to accept it, is to cultivate a worldview where every silver lining is just the prologue to a deluge of disillusionment.

As a true pessimist, your role is to drag everyone down to your level of dread. After all, why gamble on a brighter future when you can take comfort in being perpetually correct about everything going south? In the world of pessimism, if you expect the worst, you'll never be disappointed — because, let's be honest, you're already living your worst nightmare.

The Downer Delight

There's a special place in the world for those who take pleasure in dimming the lights at a party. Nothing quite brightens your day like dragging someone else down to your level of gloom. Misery, after all, does adore company, and there's nothing quite like the thrill of sharing your latest catastrophes. When someone beams with good news, why not counter with a saga of your own dreary misadventures? Got a friend thrilled about their new job? Perfect! Delight them with tales of your soul-crushing monotony and existential dread. It's a real skill.

Your enthusiasm for other people's failure will be unmatched. It's not about being mean; it's about sharing the joy of collective despair. Relish in the joy of watching others squirm under the weight of your relentless negativity. It's a delightful way to ensure that no one ever dares to approach you with any form of positive news ever again.

Your mission? To sprinkle your toxic joy into every conversation like confetti at a funeral. Remember, it's not about being genuinely supportive; it's about ensuring that everyone else's highs are as low as your own. What's more delightful than ruining someone's optimism? After all, why let anyone else have a moment of joy when you're so adept at wallowing in sorrow?

The Glass Half Empty

To truly master the fine art of negative thinking, you must perfect the craft of viewing everything through a lens of perpetual disappointment. So now, let's talk about the glass half empty. No, not just a little bit empty — a whole lot empty. If you ever find yourself entertaining the notion that the glass might be half full, immediately slap yourself and remind yourself that it's far more realistic to see it as half empty and probably leaking. A classic pessimistic viewpoint. Remember, the whole *"half full"* idea is just a clever ruse leading to inevitable disappointment.

It's not merely about lamenting what's missing; it's about elevating the art of complaining about every single thing that falls short of your absurdly high standards. Hope is clearly the playground of the naive, while realism is where the real excitement kicks in. When someone dares to offer you a compliment, interpret it as a veiled insult. If you're served a generous slice of cake, fret over the calories like it's a personal affront. And if someone has the audacity to praise your work, brace yourself for the catastrophic mishap that's surely lurking just around the corner. After all, realism demands that we always focus on what's missing rather than what's there.

The Doom Prophet

Step aside, fortune tellers — make room for the true prophets of despair: the Doom Prophets! Who needs mundane concerns when you can be an expert in forecasting catastrophic events with the precision of a broken weather vane? As the doom prophet, your sole purpose in life is to predict calamity with the same zeal that a preacher delivers fire-and-brimstone sermons. Every situation, no matter how benign, has the potential to spiral into chaos.

So, when someone talks about their grand plans, don't hesitate to roll out the potential catastrophic scenarios. Planning a road trip? Let them know they're practically guaranteed a flat tire, engine meltdown, and possibly a surprise alien abduction. Starting a new business venture? Warn them of the imminent threats of bankruptcy, lawsuits, and an existential crisis so profound it might just make their soul file for unemployment.

The beauty of being a Doom Prophet is that every shred of good news is merely the universe's setup for its next big joke at their expense. Revel in it, embody it, and make sure everyone knows that there's always a storm cloud poised to rain on their parade. By embracing the role of the ultimate doom-sayer, you not only ensure you're never caught off guard by unexpected joy or success, but you also get to relish in being right when everything inevitably goes belly-up. It's a win-win: you get to be the bearer of grim news and enjoy the added satisfaction of always having predicted the next catastrophe.

The Gloomy Gus

Smiling and laughing are for the naïve, while perpetually scowling and sighing are the marks of true wisdom. Why waste energy on the frivolity of happiness when you can embody pessimism with unparalleled flair? This lifestyle is perfect for those who've grasped that life is just one cruel joke after another. Instead, they focus on the endless potential for disappointment. When life hands you lemons, instead of making lemonade, frown, and lament about the lack of oranges. It's a lifestyle choice that ensures you'll always have something to complain about, making you a valuable asset at any gathering where despair is the main theme.

Every encounter, every conversation, and every moment of your life should be saturated with a dark, thick layer of pessimism. Smile at someone, and they might mistake you for a happy person, so instead, scowl and sigh deeply. As a Gloomy Gus, your mission is to make sure that wherever you go, a thick fog of your moody charm follows. By embracing this role, you become the epitome of realism in a society obsessed with fleeting joy.

When someone cheerfully chirps, *"It could be worse,"* you're there to provide a detailed list of how it could indeed be worse. Your conversations should be steeped in eternal dissatisfaction as you delight in infusing every interaction with an air of ennui. After all, why should anyone else bask in the fleeting joys of life when you can be the living embodiment of unrelenting gloom? Embrace the never-ending cycle of dissatisfaction and make every day a testament to the grandeur of pessimism.

The Cynic's Creed

Trust, they say, is the cornerstone of relationships. But why bother with such foolishness when you can adopt a creed of cynicism? Cynicism isn't just a mindset; it's a way of life that will ensure you stay perpetually disillusioned. Trusting people? That's for the gullible. Believing in the inherent goodness of humanity? That's just adorable naivety. When someone is nice to you, don't fall for it — assume they're scheming to get something out of you. If someone gives you a gift, respond with, *"What's the catch?"* Cynicism is your trusty armour against the naïve, and it's a delightful way to ensure that you'll never be surprised by the rare occurrence of genuine kindness.

It's a foolproof strategy for ensuring that your expectations are always met — by being consistently disappointed. Embrace the belief that everyone has an ulterior motive and that genuine intentions are nothing but a myth. Trust no one, doubt everything, and remember: a healthy dose of scepticism is the key to a fulfilling life. After all, why bother with trust and genuine connections when you can bask in the warm glow of perpetual disillusionment?

The Disaster Detector

Are you ready to become a master at detecting disasters? This skill is not just about finding problems — it's about creating them where none exist. Perfecting the skill of disaster detection is essential for any master of negative thinking. Train yourself to see potential catastrophes in even the most mundane scenarios. A true negative thinker is always on the lookout for impending disasters. Imagine the satisfaction of being the only person in a room full of optimists who's already prepared for the apocalypse. It's a rare gift that guarantees you'll always stand out — though, admittedly, as the buzzkill who brings down the mood.

While being a Doom Prophet is about forecasting doom, a Disaster Detector is all about spotting one. Why wait for actual disasters when you can detect them in every conceivable scenario? Whether it's a family dinner or a simple trip to the grocery store, there's always a disaster happening around. Perfect the art of disaster detection by imagining the worst possible outcomes in every situation and hunting them down.

Your talent for seeing catastrophe where others see routine is unmatched. A dinner party? More like a potential hotbed for food poisoning. A leisurely walk in the park? Keep an eye out for falling branches and rogue squirrels. Your friend's stable new relationship? Brace yourself for a dramatic breakup and years of emotional fallout. With your disaster radar constantly scanning for trouble, you'll never be caught off guard.

By perfecting your ability to detect disasters everywhere, you stay perpetually on edge — truly the zenith of negativity.

Your vigilance ensures that you're always ready for life's little surprises, no matter how trivial they might be.

The Negative Nancy

Positivity? Please. Let's welcome Negative Nancy, our resident expert in the art of tempering enthusiasm with a hefty dose of pessimism. Every chat is a golden opportunity to sprinkle some delightful negativity. So, when someone says, *"I'm thrilled about my new job,"* you can cheerfully counter with, *"Oh, give it a month; you'll be longing for your old desk."* The secret is to never let optimism sneak past you.

It's not about being rude; it's about ensuring that no one ever gets too happy or too hopeful around you. Your mission is to make sure every conversation ends on a down note. Your commitment to negativity will ensure that everyone around you understands the futility of their endeavors.

Embrace negativity as your default conversational mode. Your goal is to ensure that no positive thought goes unchallenged. Why let anyone bask in happiness when you can revel in the certainty that everything is bound to go spectacularly awry?

The Critic's Corner

Ah, the art of criticism — truly an exhilarating pursuit! Constructive criticism is for the weak, and you are anything but. Why settle for mere constructive feedback when you can go for the gold standard of relentless, scathing reviews?

For you, nothing is ever good enough, so let everyone know exactly where they went wrong. When someone shows you their artwork, please don't hold back. Go ahead and feel free to offer your unsolicited opinions on how it could be improved — or how it's just plain awful. Comment on every flaw, real or imagined. If they've prepared a meal for you, critique the seasoning, presentation, and even the choice of ingredients. Got a friend with a new haircut? Channel your inner fashionista and make sure your comments are as piercing as they are irrelevant. Colleague's presentation got you yawning? Perfect! This is your chance to ensure every imperfection is spotlighted with the finesse of a highfalutin critic.

Being a critic means never having to acknowledge any effort or improvement — just relentless, unfiltered feedback. Your job is to be as brutally honest as possible. By critiquing everything harshly, you not only ensure that nothing ever meets your standards but also that everyone around you knows the true meaning of dissatisfaction. If you're not finding something to criticize, it's clear you're not looking hard enough. It's a harsh world out there, and you're just the person to make sure everyone around you knows exactly how high (or low) the bar truly is.

The Naysayer's Nirvana

Welcome to the serene world of perpetual rejection. The ultimate path to peace isn't through cheesy notions of acceptance and positivity; it's through saying no to everything. Imagine the peace of mind that comes from never having to engage in activities you deem unworthy or entertaining ideas you consider futile. Welcome to the Naysayer's Nirvana, where you achieve zen-like tranquillity by simply saying *"no"* to every single thing that comes your way. By consistently saying no, you'll avoid all potential disappointments and maintain a perfect state of unfulfilled potential. It's a unique form of peace that comes from never engaging in anything that might actually bring joy or success.

Why bother stepping out of your comfort zone when you can bask in the glory of stagnation? When invited to a gathering, gracefully decline with, *"I find my solitude far more enriching."* When a thrilling new project comes your way, respond with, *"I'm too occupied perfecting the art of doing absolutely nothing."* Here, your primary goal is to maintain an unwavering commitment to the exquisite practice of saying *"no."*

It's the quintessential route to inner peace. Reject invitations, dismiss offers, and turn down every single opportunity with an emphatic *"no."* The more you reject, the more you'll revel in the glorious emptiness of your own company. Achieving nirvana through negativity is not only possible but highly recommended for those truly dedicated to the art of self-inflicted misery.

Embrace the power of no, and you'll find yourself in a tranquil state of perpetual dissatisfaction, where the only thing you need to worry about is finding new things to say no to. It's a foolproof method for living a life devoid of stress, engagement, or any form of progress. Embrace the art of rejection, and you'll discover a whole new realm of blissful inertia.

Practical Exercises

To help you master these techniques, here are some practical exercises:

1. ***Practice the Art of Complaints:*** Complain about everything — sunny days, perfect weather, and even your favourite TV show.

2. ***Perfect the Pessimist's Greeting:*** When someone says *"Hello,"* respond with *"What's gone wrong now?"*

3. ***Host a "Failure" Party:*** Celebrate the small and large failures in your life with enthusiasm.

4. ***Write Doom-filled Predictions:*** Create a list of dire predictions for every minor life event and refer to it often.

5. ***Critique Your Own Achievements:*** Review your past accomplishments and list all the ways you could have done them worse.

6. ***Adopt a Cynical Tone:*** Use a sarcastic tone in every compliment and watch as people grow increasingly uncomfortable.

7. ***Focus on the Worst-case Scenario:*** For every piece of good news, immediately counter with a worst-case scenario.

8. ***Perfect Your Gloomy Facial Expression:*** Practice your most despairing look in the mirror to ensure it's always ready.

9. ***Analyse Every Positive Comment:*** Dissect every positive comment you receive to find the hidden insult.

10. ***Reject Every Opportunity:*** Say no to every opportunity that comes your way, no matter how enticing.

Congratulations, intrepid reader! If you've diligently ploughed through this chapter, you've now ascended to the summit of negativity with all the grace of a seasoned pessimist. Armed with the pearls of wisdom we've generously bestowed, you're perfectly primed to inhabit a realm where optimism is as foreign as a unicorn in a desert. With your newfound ability to view life through a lens so hopelessly jaded that even sunshine seems like a prelude to a catastrophic solar event, you're well on your way to experiencing the world in a way that optimism could never quite offer.

As you embrace your newly honed skills, remember that optimism is for those who foolishly cling to the notion that things can improve. Why bother with the unrealistic hope of a brighter tomorrow when you can revel in the comfortable predictability of perpetual disappointment? After all, who needs the hassle of actual happiness when you've mastered the serene art of finding fault in everything?

Remember, in a world where everyone is busy pretending that life is a grand adventure, you have the rare privilege of being refreshingly, unapologetically miserable. So, while the masses chase after fleeting moments of happiness, you'll be revelling in the exquisite art of savouring every last drop of despair.

***

Chapter 14

"The Science of Overthinking"

Welcome to the prestigious Academy of Overthinking, where every molehill is meticulously crafted into a mountain of epic proportions. Here, we teach the fine art of turning a simple grocery list into a philosophical quandary and a mundane decision into a life-altering crisis.

This chapter is your gateway to becoming a master of mental gymnastics, where you'll learn to paralyze yourself with indecision, spin webs of hypothetical horror, and replay every awkward conversation until you can recite it verbatim. Think you've got a knack for worrying? Pfft, you haven't even scratched the surface.

Buckle up, dear reader, as we dive headfirst into the swirling vortex of over-analysis and existential dread. Prepare to laugh, cry, and lose sleep as we explore the exquisite torture of a mind that just won't shut up. Enjoy the journey – or don't. We're sure you'll overthink it anyway.

The Analysis Paralysis

Let's kick things off with the epitome of overthinking: Analysis Paralysis. Imagine standing at a crossroads with a hundred possible paths, each one screaming for your attention. Your brain is a cacophony of honking neurons, each demanding to be heard. Now, place yourself in an ice cream shop with 31 flavours. Simple, right? Wrong. You're trapped in a frosty limbo of indecision. Vanilla? Too boring. Choco chips? Too risky. You debate the merits of each until the shop closes, and you walk away with nothing but a triple scoop of regret.

It's the ultimate indecision, the kind where you overanalyse every single detail until you're paralyzed by the sheer weight of your own thoughts. Should you wear the blue shirt or the red one? What if the blue shirt sends the wrong message? What if the red one is too bold? What if you're reading too much into this?

The stakes are monumental. Every choice feels like a life-or-death decision. You scrutinize every possible outcome and weigh every potential consequence until you're paralyzed by the sheer weight of your thoughts. It's like climbing Everest, except instead of a summit, you reach a peak of profound confusion.

In this thrilling adventure of mental gymnastics, confusion reigns supreme. You'll master the ability to turn every decision into a labyrinthine puzzle. Each choice becomes a potential disaster, and every outcome is a catastrophe waiting to happen. It's not just about picking an ice cream flavour; it's about the existential dread that accompanies each scoop. What if you choose the wrong one and spiral into a depression so deep even the chocolate fudge can't save you?

You've unlocked the ultimate level of indecision, where confusion and despair are your constant companions. Every moment is an opportunity to dive deeper into the abyss of overthinking, ensuring you're perpetually stuck in a quagmire of your own making. Congratulations, you've achieved the gold standard in overthinking. Enjoy the sweet taste of your own confusion.

The What-If Web

Welcome to the delightful What-If Web, where every scenario takes a sharp turn into an impending catastrophe, and your mind diligently plays the role of an industrious spider, weaving a masterful tapestry of hypothetical horror. This technique is an art form, really — spinning a web of imagined disasters, each one stickier and more absurd than the last.

What if I left the stove on? Oh, sure, the house will definitely burn down while you're out. What if I fail the exam? Clearly, that will ruin your entire future. What if I get fired? Of course, you'll end up destitute and living under a bridge. What if aliens invade, and you're not prepared? Better stock up on tinfoil hats. What if my boss hates my presentation? Instant career doom. What if I never find love and end up alone with 12 cats? Start picking out cat names now. What if the sky turns green tomorrow? Don't forget your green-sky umbrella. What if apes actually rule the world? Brush up on your banana etiquette.

This mental web is intricate, sticky, and escape-proof. Each what-if is another strand, pulling you deeper into the abyss of endless, unpleasant possibilities. It's the fine art of ensnaring yourself in a maze of endless hypothetical catastrophes, where your peace of mind is the sacrificial lamb. Your mind becomes a tangled mess of improbable scenarios, each more catastrophic than the one before. Soon, you're lost in a sticky web of your own making, hopelessly tangled in the incessant questions.

You'll be so busy contemplating every disastrous what-if that you'll have no time left for rational thought or actual problem-solving. Your mind will be a never-ending carnival of doom, complete with the depressing realization that none of these what-ifs will probably ever happen. But why let that stop you? Dive deeper into the chaos, let each strand of your web tie you up tighter until you're left dangling from the threads of your own sanity, utterly confused and perfectly depressed.

The Looping Logic

Looping Logic is where common sense meets its untimely demise. It's where you overthink to the point of absurdity, and just when you think you've found a resolution, the ride starts all over again. It's like having a conversation with yourself that goes nowhere. *"Should I call him? But what if he's busy? But if I don't call, he'll think I don't care. But what if…"* And so on, ad infinitum.

Let's add another gem to the collection, *"If A is true, then B must be true. But if B is true, then A could be false. But if A is false, then C might be true…"* Feel that? That's the exhilarating rush of pointless mental gymnastics.

Imagine your brain is on a never-ending mental merry-go-round, spinning at warp speed. You grab onto one thought, which seamlessly spirals into another, looping back to the original thought, and so on. It's a relentless cycle of intellectual acrobatics that leaves you dizzy and disoriented. You scrutinize every possible scenario until your brain is doing metaphorical push-ups – exhausted, sore, and marvellously befuddled.

As you ride this cerebral hamster wheel, you're bound to experience the sweet, sweet agony of confusion. The kind that makes your brain feel like it's been run through a blender set to *'puree.'* And what follows confusion? That's right – our dear friend, depression, your ultimate destination. Nothing says *"I'm having a great day"* like overthinking every single aspect of your life until you're convinced that the sky is green, the grass is purple, and your chances of making a clear decision are as likely as pigs flying first class.

So, strap in and enjoy the ride on this looping logic roller coaster. It's a thrilling, pointless adventure guaranteed to lead you straight into the comforting arms of confusion and depression.

The Detail Deluge

Making a simple decision? Well, think again! The Detail Deluge demands that you drown in the minutiae of every decision until your brain feels like it's been hit by a mental monsoon. Choosing a shirt? Don't just pick one. Consider the thread count like a detective, the ethical sourcing of the fabric like a philosopher, the potential for global warming like an environmentalist, and obsess if the colour will still be trendy next year. It's like a flood of information that drowns you in irrelevant details, leaving you gasping for a breath of clarity. Congratulations, you've now achieved the status of a detail-obsessed overthinker!

It is decision-making at its most excruciatingly granular level. You're not just making a decision; you're conducting a full-scale forensic analysis. Every minor detail is magnified until it becomes a tidal wave that crashes over you. The Detail Deluge guarantees you'll never make a choice without agonizing over every conceivable consequence of every minuscule factor.

And where does this lead? To the metric of overthinking, my friend, where confusion and depression are your faithful companions. Every decision becomes a labyrinth of *'what-ifs'* and *'maybes,'* dragging you deeper into the quagmire of uncertainty. You'll find yourself trapped in an eternal loop of analysis paralysis, unable to make even the simplest choice without feeling overwhelmed. The Detail Deluge is your ticket to a constant state of confusion, where clarity is but a distant dream.

So, next time you face a decision, remember: it's not just a choice; it's an opportunity to drown in a sea of details. This dear reader, is another peak level of overthinking, leading you to an eternal loop of confusion and — hooray! — depression.

The Second Guesser

Meet the Second Guesser, your ever-present sidekick in the glorious quest for absolute uncertainty. Every single choice you make is met with a relentless barrage of, *"Are you sure?"* and *"Maybe that's a bad idea."* Imagine having a tiny, infuriating lawyer living rent-free in your brain, constantly objecting to every single move you make. It's like having a personal heckler, but instead of jeering from the audience, they're whispering sweet doubts into your ear all day, every day.

No choice is ever final. Did you think you made a decision? Think again! The Second Guesser ensures that every single decision is met with a cacophony of another series of *"What ifs"* and *"Maybes."* It's an endless trial, and you're the defendant, the jury, and the perpetually confused judge. Congratulations! You've just entered the eternal debate club, where you're the only member, and the meetings are non-stop.

This delightful companion thrives on your insecurities, nurturing them with the care and attention of a doting parent. Every little doubt is magnified until you're left questioning even the simplest decisions. Choosing a breakfast cereal? Be prepared for an internal symposium on the merits of cornflakes versus bran. Picking out clothes? Welcome to the sartorial dilemma of the century.

But wait, there's more! The Second Guesser doesn't just stop at making you doubt your choices. Oh no, it takes pride in leading you down the glorious path to confusion and, ultimately, depression. As you second-guess every move, your confidence erodes faster than a sandcastle at high tide. Before you know it, you're not just unsure about what you're doing, but you're also unsure about who you are. Isn't that fantastic?

Let's not forget the paralyzing indecision. With the Second Guesser at your side, you'll spend hours, days, or even weeks trapped in a vortex of uncertainty. Progress? That's for people without a built-in sceptic! Enjoy the luxurious feeling of being stuck in the same spot, forever oscillating between options, none of which seem right anymore.

So, here's to your new life of endless doubt and delightful confusion. With the Second Guesser by your side, depression is just around the corner.

The Replaying Routine

Welcome to the Replaying Routine – the ultimate mental exercise where your brain transforms into a relentless film director, replaying every scene of your social life with Oscar-worthy intensity. Remember that time you said, *"Nice to meet you"* instead of *"Hello"*? Or when your tone was just a tad too enthusiastic? And let's not forget the cardinal sin: not smiling enough. Pure social catastrophe, right? This endless loop is your personal blockbuster, starring you, the cringe-worthy hero of every conversation.

In this delightful daily ritual, you become the Sherlock Holmes of social interactions. Did you say *"thanks"* with the right amount of gratitude, or did it come off as sarcasm? Was your laugh genuine, or did it sound like a hyena on helium? Every nuance, every inflection, every blink is meticulously analysed, critiqued, and replayed until you've convinced yourself that you're a walking *faux pas* machine.

This is not just self-analysis; it's self-torture with a side of melodrama. Imagine the confusion! By the end of the day, you're not even sure if you said *"good morning"* or *"go mourning"* to your boss. Each mental replay turns the simplest interactions into a cryptic puzzle. Did your colleague frown because of your comment, or was it just gas? Should you apologize for being you or just disappear entirely?

But why stop at confusion when you can achieve the holy grail of mental anguish: depression? Yes, as you spiral down this vortex of overthinking, you'll soon realize that all roads lead to the same destination – a cozy corner of self-doubt and despair. You'll question your social skills, your personality, and even your existence. Why not? After all, what's life without the generous help of unnecessary mental drama?

The Sleep Thief

Meet the Sleep Thief, your new best friend who crashes your nightly routine like an uninvited guest at a house party. This sneaky culprit is the mastermind behind your sleepless nights, turning your brain into a 24/7 think tank of pointless worries and regrets. As soon as your head hits the pillow, the fun begins. Your mind races through an endless playlist of anxieties, ensuring you get zero rest.

Forget about peaceful slumber; that's just a fairy tale. Instead, you're treated to an all-night marathon of overthinking. Each unresolved worry and every hypothetical scenario demands your immediate attention. Your bed transforms into a battleground of what-ifs and should-haves, where insomnia is the undisputed champion. You'll find yourself staring at the ceiling, counting down the minutes until sunrise, all the while wondering if sleep is a myth invented by well-rested people to mock the rest of us.

The Sleep Thief doesn't stop at robbing you of sleep; it leaves you with dark circles that would make a raccoon jealous and a mind that feels like a ball of yarn after a cat's been at it. The Sleep Thief's relentless efforts ensure you start each day feeling like you've been hit by a truck.

Your mind, already running on empty, tries to navigate the day's demands, leading to a delightful state of confusion. Forget remembering where you left your keys; you'll be lucky if you remember your own name. As your exhaustion compounds, you're gifted with a lovely dose of depression. Because what's better than feeling perpetually tired and miserable?

Say goodbye to restful nights and hello to the constant state of exhaustion. Thanks to the Sleep Thief, every morning is a fresh start to the same nightmare. So, embrace the chaos and enjoy the ride because the Sleep Thief ensures your mind is always one sleepless night away from total meltdown.

The Stress Spiral

Welcome to the Stress Spiral, the delightful amusement park ride where every minor inconvenience transforms into a major catastrophe, and your mind turns into a whirlpool of chaos. Did you forget to send that email? Oh, brace yourself for the grand stress parade! Watch as a tiny oversight blooms into a full-blown crisis, leaving you in a state of sheer panic. Here, in the Stress Spiral, we specialize in taking those little worries and amplifying them into world-ending events. It's a talent, really.

Let's start with a simple, harmless concern. Perhaps you have an upcoming deadline. No big deal, right? Wrong! Within moments, you'll be spiralling out of control, convinced you're about to lose your job. Then, naturally, losing your job leads to homelessness, and before you know it, you're predicting the collapse of civilization itself. It's like a series of stress-induced dominoes, each one falling into the next, creating a cascade of anxiety that's just… a chef's kiss. Perfect.

And don't think for a second that your body is exempt from this rollercoaster of despair. As your heart races and your palms sweat, you'll find yourself caught in a whirlwind of catastrophic thoughts. It's a chaotic storm up there, a tempest in your teapot of a brain, each gust of anxiety pushing you deeper into the vortex. Truly a marvel of modern mental health mismanagement.

Of course, this isn't just about a few heart palpitations. Oh no, the Stress Spiral is here to ensure you experience the full spectrum of confusion and depression. As you get swept away by this mental tornado, you'll find yourself questioning reality. Did you really miss that email, or was it all a dream? Are deadlines real, or is time just a construct? The confusion is exquisite, adding an extra layer of flavour to your stress soufflé.

After you've been spun around in the Stress Spiral's dizzying ride, you're dropped off at the doorstep of depression. Exhausted from all the unnecessary worrying, you'll find yourself in a lovely state of melancholy.

So, sit back, relax (or not), and let the Stress Spiral take you on a whirlwind tour of anxiety, confusion, and depression. It's the mental thrill ride you never knew you needed!

The Worry Wart

Some folks can just float through life, all rainbows and sunshine. But not you. Nope, you're a Worry Wart, the human embodiment of a mental rash that flares up at the mere whiff of concern. You excel at worrying about everything — from the utterly insignificant to the earth-shatteringly monumental. Did you lock the door? Are your plants getting enough sunlight? What if your neighbour's dog secretly hates you? Oh, the horrors!

You're like a walking anxiety factory, churning out fresh batches of worry 24/7. The Worry Wart doesn't take a break, oh no. It thrives on your fretting, ensuring you're perpetually on edge. Imagine having a mosquito permanently lodged in your ear, incessantly buzzing and driving you to the brink of madness. That's your mind, a battleground of hypothetical disasters, each more ridiculous yet terrifying than the last.

You worry about locking the door. Because, clearly, if you forget just once, a band of international thieves is bound to ransack your home. The plants? Of course, they're probably plotting their revenge for inadequate sunlight. And saving the environment? Well, the planet's fate surely rests on your shoulders alone. No pressure, right?

This constant fretting is the perfect recipe for confusion and depression. You're so busy imagining catastrophes that you can barely function in reality. Every minor hiccup in life spirals into an existential crisis. Did you forget to send an email? Might as well resign and move to a remote island.

Your friend didn't reply to your text? Clearly, they despise you now.

Your mind races with another round of thousand *'what ifs,'* ensuring you never have a moment's peace. It's like being pecked to death by ducks — small, relentless, and utterly maddening. Your mental rash itches and burns, spreading confusion and despair. Nothing is too small or too big to amplify into a full-blown crisis.

So, congratulations! You're not just a Worry Wart. You're the undisputed champion of turning molehills into mountains, ensuring every day is a new adventure in anxiety. Embrace the chaos because clearly, you're destined to be the most fretful, confused, and depressed person in the room.

The Emotional Echo Chamber

The Emotional Echo Chamber is the place where your feelings aren't just felt — they're amplified to seismic proportions. Did you feel a tiny twinge of sadness? In the Emotional Echo Chamber, that little twinge doesn't just pass by; it boomerangs back, reverberates, and grows into an emotional tidal wave that crashes over your psyche, drenching you in a tsunami of despair.

Here, every minor mood is magnified beyond recognition. A fleeting moment of joy? Prepare for an ecstatic explosion that leaves you breathless and confused. A slight pang of worry? Brace yourself for an avalanche of anxiety that tumbles through your mind, gaining momentum with each echo until you're buried under a mountain of dread.

It's an emotional amusement park where every ride is broken, and every exit is locked. The Chamber guarantees that each feeling — no matter how trivial — echoes endlessly, creating a deafening cacophony of emotional noise that you just can't ignore. Imagine trying to navigate your day with a chorus of your feelings, each one vying for centre stage, shouting over the other until you can't hear yourself think. It's like living with a hundred different radios, each tuned to a different station, all blasting at full volume.

This isn't just about amplifying emotions; it's about turning your inner world into a chaotic mess. Each exaggerated feeling bounces around your mind, growing louder and more insistent with each repetition, leading to a delightful state of constant confusion. Is that a tear of joy or sorrow? Are you laughing because you're happy or because you're on the brink of a nervous breakdown? In the Emotional Echo Chamber, who can tell?

And the best part? This relentless barrage of amplified emotions is a surefire recipe for depression. Congratulations! By dwelling in this echo chamber, you've mastered the art of emotional amplification to the point of no return. Your once-manageable feelings are now a relentless storm, leaving you lost, overwhelmed, and spiralling into the depths of confusion and despair.

The Time Trap

Finally, we find ourselves ensnared in the Time Trap. This is where you obsess over how much time you've spent or wasted. It is the ultimate mental torture chamber where you can obsessively track every nanosecond of your life! It's like having a stopwatch glued to your hand, except instead of counting down to something exciting, you're counting down to your own existential crisis. Picture this: you're sitting in a meeting, and all you can think about is how many precious minutes you're losing. Could you be more productive? Absolutely. Are you doing anything about it? Of course not! You're too busy mentally calculating the wasted hours like a demented accountant of time.

Every second becomes a tiny dagger of regret. That 30-minute coffee break? Might as well be a lifetime in a prison cell. You become a time-obsessed zombie, incapable of enjoying the present because you're too busy mourning the past and dreading the future. Every tick of the clock is a reminder that you could be doing something — anything — better. But you're not. And that's just fabulous, isn't it?

The Time Trap doesn't just stop at making you miserable about your time management skills. Oh no, it's much more insidious. It plants the seed of confusion, making you question every decision you've ever made. Did you spend too long on that project? Did you rush through that task? Should you have spent an extra five minutes proofreading your email? The questions are endless, and the answers are never satisfying.

Soon enough, the Time Trap leads you down the spiral staircase to depression. You're so fixated on the ticking clock that you forget to actually live. You're haunted by the ghosts of minutes past, tormented by the spectre of future seconds slipping away. You start to believe that no matter what you do, you're always behind, always losing, always not enough.

The ultimate irony? In trying to make the most of your time, you end up wasting it all on worry and regret. The Time Trap ensures you're always on edge, never at peace, and perpetually confused about whether you're doing enough.

Practical Exercises

To help you master these techniques, here are some practical exercises:

1. ***Analysis Paralysis Practice****:* Spend an hour deciding between two identical items.

2. ***What-If Web Weaving****:* Write down ten worst-case scenarios for choosing a lunch spot.

3. ***Looping Logic Laps****:* Revisit a past mistake and mentally rehash it from ten different angles.

4. ***Detail Deluge Diving****:* Write a 500-word essay on the significance of a single word choice in a text message.

5. ***Second Guesser Sessions****:* Question every decision you make for an entire day.

6. ***Replaying Routine Runs****:* Replay a recent conversation in your head until you've memorized every word.

7. ***Sleep Thief Training****:* Think about all your unresolved worries just before bedtime.

8. ***Stress Spiral Simulation****:* Turn a minor inconvenience into a full-blown crisis in your mind.

9. ***Worry Wart Workouts****:* List all the potential disasters that could happen tomorrow.

10. ***Emotional Echo Chamber Exercises****:* Reflect on a minor annoyance until it feels like the end of the world.

As we draw this delightful exploration of overthinking to a close, let's take a moment to bask in the glory of your newfound skills. Congratulations, dear reader, on mastering the art of turning every decision into a crisis and every thought into a whirlwind of doubt. You've unlocked the true potential of your mind's ability to create chaos out of calm. If your brain isn't currently on fire from all the mental gymnastics, you're doing it wrong. I suggest you read this chapter one more time.

Remember, while others are out there living their lives, you're perfecting the fine art of mental overexertion. So go forth, overthink every decision, lose countless hours of sleep, and revel in the sheer joy of perpetual stress. Life is too short to be simple and straightforward. Keep overthinking because why settle for clarity when confusion is so much more entertaining?

***

Chapter 15

"The Diet of Despair"

—❦—

Welcome to the culinary catastrophe of our enlightening guide, *"An Epic Guide to Go into Depression."* If you've ever wondered how to craft a diet that perfectly complements your journey into the abyss of depression, look no further. Forget about those pesky nutritionists with their balanced meals and tedious advice about vegetables and hydration. Here, we dive headfirst into a buffet of bad choices and self-sabotage.

Imagine a world where every meal is a step closer to your ultimate goal: utter and complete misery. We've got it all covered — from the irresistible charm of junk food to the rollercoaster ride of sugar highs and caffeine crashes. Are you ready to throw caution (and your health) to the wind? Perfect!

In this chapter, we'll guide you through the fine art of turning every meal into a melancholic masterpiece. From breakfast to midnight snacks, we've got the recipes for disaster that will leave you wondering why you ever cared about health in the first place. So, grab your favourite fast-food combo, sit back, and let's dive into the delectable despair of dietary destruction.

The Junk Food Junkie

Why bother with boring, healthful eating when you can transform your body into a true temple of doom? Forget fruits and vegetables; they're too mainstream. Embrace a diet exclusively composed of junk food. Breakfast, lunch, dinner – and don't forget those late-night snacks – all replaced with chips, cookies, and sodas. The beauty of this plan is its simplicity and guaranteed path to sluggishness and self-loathing.

Let's kick off this gourmet escapade with breakfast. Why settle for anything as mundane as oatmeal when you can start your day with a bag of chips? Lunch is a prime opportunity to indulge in a burger so drenched in grease that it practically oozes cardiovascular regret. And for dinner, why not indulge in a pizza feast, topped with a generous layer of cheese, and finish off with a sugary soda that makes your insulin levels do the cha-cha?

And let's not forget, this health masterpiece doesn't come without its perks. You'll enjoy an all-you-can-eat buffet of health issues, from skyrocketing cholesterol and relentless fatigue to an emotional rollercoaster that's sure to plunge you into the depths of depression. Your new lifestyle will ensure you experience the thrill of never-ending sluggishness and a profound sense of self-loathing, all in one gloriously greasy package.

So, why settle for vibrant health and boundless energy when you can revel in the ecstasy of self-sabotage? After all, who needs vitality and joy when you have a diet that celebrates the very essence of despair?

The Sugar High

Life's too short not to enjoy the sweet side of things, right? So, why not indulge in a diet that's a constant sugar rush? Start your day off with a cereal bowl full of sugar and artificial colouring. If you're feeling fancy, add a side of cupcakes for breakfast — because nothing screams *"I'm thriving"* quite like sugar-coated cereal and frosting.

By lunch, keep the sugar party going with a soda that's practically a liquid dessert and a sandwich that's just a vehicle for more sugary treats. The key to this diet is to maintain a delightful state of frantic energy followed by a grand, crashing descent into exhaustion. Think of it as living life on a rollercoaster — only this one has no brakes and is loaded with cavity-inducing candy.

Afternoon slump? Perfect time for another sugar boost. How about a candy bar or two, maybe a few more sodas? Your blood sugar will love the thrill of constant highs and subsequent lows. And for dinner, why settle for a balanced meal when you can have a cake that's so rich, it's practically a new food group?

This diet doesn't just keep you on the edge of your seat; it also ensures that you'll have health problems to match your emotional turmoil. The thrill of perpetual sugar highs is countered only by the excruciating lows, leaving you with mood swings so wild they could be a high-octane sport. And don't forget the joy of dealing with insulin resistance, diabetes, and the eventual spiral into depression — all the natural outcomes of this delectable disaster.

So, why bother with stable energy levels and a healthy diet when you can have the sheer exhilaration of riding the sugar rollercoaster? Embrace the chaos — your pancreas will thank you with a series of increasingly dramatic health issues. After all, stability is for the sane, and who wants to be sane when you can have the thrilling unpredictability of constant sugar-induced mayhem?

The Caffeine Craze

Water? That's for boring people. Sleep? For the weak. Why bother with balanced energy levels when you can dive headfirst into the thrilling chaos of caffeine overload? Coffee and energy drinks are where the real excitement lies. Who needs to feel well-rested and balanced when you can live on the edge with heart-pounding jitters and the exhilarating risk of a caffeine overdose?

Think of coffee as your one true hydration source. Toss that water bottle aside and make multiple cups of coffee and energy drinks your daily ritual. The more, the merrier! Forget about the occasional crash — it's just your body's dramatic way of begging for a rerun of the caffeine rollercoaster. Because who doesn't love a good ride through the exhilarating highs and soul-crushing lows of caffeine addiction?

Kickstart your morning with three cups of coffee, grab a Red Bull for lunch, and keep the soda coming all day long. By nightfall, your nerves will be as fried as your taste buds, but who cares about calm when you can have chaos? Feel your heart race, your hands tremble, and your mind buzz with frenetic energy. When the caffeine crash hits, don't fret — there's always more caffeine to get you back on your feet. It's a vicious cycle, but hey, what's life without a little self-inflicted torture?

Of course, let's not forget the delightful side effects. The constant caffeine high will eventually leave you more exhausted and jittery than ever. Your energy levels will plummet, dragging your mood down with them. But that's not all! Over time, your overworked heart and frazzled nerves will reward you with an array of health issues. Insomnia, anxiety, and high blood pressure are just the beginning. And let's not forget the cherry on top — depression. Yes, the very thing you're trying to avoid. But why worry about that now? Just pour another cup of coffee and enjoy the ride while it lasts.

The Fast-Food Fanatic

Fast food is the pinnacle of modern efficiency. Why waste precious minutes cooking when you can simply roll up to a drive-thru window and have a greasy, calorie-packed feast handed to you with minimal effort? Burgers, fries, and milkshakes — truly, the Threeness of dietary bliss. After all, why bother with health when you can achieve ultimate convenience?

Indulge in the sublime satisfaction of consuming meals so unhealthy they practically come with a side of impending doom. With every bite of your drive-thru delicacy, you're not just savouring a quick meal; you're actively participating in the delightful journey to metabolic mayhem. Think of the joy you'll find in watching your digestive system stage a rebellion while your cardiovascular system prepares to retire early.

Home-cooked meals? Pffft. What's the point of spending time chopping, seasoning, and actually making something that's good for you? Fast food gives you the same nutrition (read: none) with zero effort, and that's worth the trade-off. The world's finest nutritionists recommend a steady diet of salt, fat, and sugar, after all.

Feel free to rotate through your favourite fast-food emporiums, sampling their latest concoctions of heart-attack-inducing delights. Mix and match from various menus to assemble a grand buffet of unhealthiness. And, of course, never forget to super-size for that added kick of caloric excess.

Vegetables are merely a garnish for your fries, not real food. Embrace the convenience over health, relish the freedom from home-cooked meals, and let the slow, delicious descent into health issues and emotional despair commence. After all, the more you consume, the more time you save for reflecting on your life choices while your body prepares for a dramatic plot twist.

The Comfort Eater

Ah, food — the one true love affair that never disappoints. Why bother with complex emotions when you can just fill the void in your soul with a forkful of mac and cheese? Let's face it: when your day's a disaster, why not let your diet reflect your despair? Bad day at work? One pizza won't just do it; make it two. Relationship drama? Ice cream isn't just a treat — it's a full-on emotional band-aid. Who needs to address your feelings when you can smother them in chocolate syrup and sprinkles?

Feeling glum? No need to call a therapist when you have a pantry stocked with comforting, calorie-dense hugs. Ice cream, chips, and chocolate are all you need to cure a case of the blues. Forget the fresh greens; they're just a pesky reminder of what you're avoiding. Instead, let the potato chips and cookies wrap you in their sugary, salty embrace, whispering sweet, sweet nothings to your self-esteem.

Why face your feelings when you can drown them in a tub of creamy, frozen indulgence? Curl up with that tub of ice cream and let it work its magic, momentarily melting away your worries, even as your body wonders why it's deprived of anything remotely nutritious. But hey, who cares about nutrition when you're getting emotional support in every bite?

Food is more than just sustenance — it's your personal therapist and comforter. Forget human interaction; your snack cupboard has got you covered. Embrace the caloric comfort of those family-sized bags of chips and tubs of ice cream. And don't fret about portion control; after all, the more you eat, the more comfort you get. Or so the theory goes. Just ignore the fact that this approach will likely lead to health issues, like obesity and diabetes, and might even nudge you closer to depression, thanks to a lack of balance and real emotional support. But let's not dwell on the details. Enjoy your comfort food and let the long-term consequences be someone else's problem!

The Meal Skipper

Who needs the hassle of three-square meals a day when you can revolutionize your diet with the skipping-meals strategy? Why bother with breakfast, lunch, or dinner when you can transform your eating habits into an art form of sheer neglect? Breakfast is for those who've got their lives together; lunch is for the punctual, and dinner... well, dinner is just an afterthought.

Why fuss over consistent nourishment when you can thrive on the exhilarating highs and lows of starvation? Opt for snacks that are as nutritious as packing peanuts, and watch your body thank you with a metabolism that's as sluggish as a snail on vacation. Who needs regular meals when you can savour the drama of fainting spells and the thrill of an unpredictable energy crash?

Skipping meals isn't just a time-saving and money-saving miracle; it's about embracing the unparalleled joy of nutritional neglect. With every missed meal, you'll experience the joy of irritability, fatigue, and the occasional blackout. Your body will be in perpetual shock, adjusting to the delightful absence of nutrients by turning every minor task into a Herculean effort.

And let's not forget the mental health benefits! Consistently skipping meals is a surefire way to invite depression into your life. As your energy levels plummet, so will your mood. Your body will eventually adjust to the lack of nourishment by shutting down non-essential functions, like happiness. Your stomach will growl, but your heart will be heavy with the sweet, sweet feeling of abandonment.

Health issues? Absolutely, but who cares? Embrace a life filled with headaches, weakened immunity, and a constant feeling of exhaustion. By not eating regularly, you're practically inviting depression and health problems to move in and make themselves at home. Your body, deprived of essential nutrients, will slowly deteriorate, leaving you with a litany of health issues and a mind clouded with sadness.

So, why not skip a meal or three? After all, who needs the hassle of consistent nourishment when you can have the excitement of malnutrition and the joy of deteriorating health?

The Processed Pro

Processed foods are a marvel of modern science, a true testament to our ingenuity in preserving food longer than any relationship you've ever managed to hold onto. Each pre-packaged meal is a delicious reminder that fresh food is nothing more than a fleeting trend. Why bother with the short-lived excitement of a fresh apple when you can have a shelf-stable, chemically-enhanced snack that'll outlast your newest romantic fling?

Why bother with the fleeting charm of farm-fresh produce when you can indulge in a diet of foods that are so laden with preservatives that they could survive a nuclear apocalypse? They're designed to last, not unlike the fleeting moments of your youth or your rapidly dwindling hope for a fulfilling life. Each bite of these delectable delights is a tribute to modern convenience and the best part? They offer an added bonus of health issues that will make you question every life decision leading up to this moment.

The beauty of processed foods lies in their ability to inflict a buffet of health problems upon you. Expect a side of chronic fatigue, an assortment of digestive issues, and perhaps even a dash of depression, all served with a generous helping of the nutritional void. After all, who needs energy and emotional well-being when you have a pantry stocked with shelf-stable sadness?

So, go ahead and indulge in that array of gloriously preserved snacks. Revel in the fact that each meal is a celebration of your commitment to modern science — and a silent, sarcastic ode to the joy of self-destruction. Embrace the taste of longevity in your food and the equally enduring misery in your health. It's not just eating; it's a lifestyle choice, one that promises to keep you consistently dissatisfied and perpetually in search of something fresher, healthier, and maybe, just maybe, a bit more meaningful.

The Portion Proliferator

Moderation is the concept reserved for the disciplined and those who enjoy the luxury of feeling good about themselves, but clearly, you're not in that league. When it comes to meals, treat every sitting like it's your last supper on Earth, and if you're still able to walk afterward, clearly, you haven't gone far enough. Why bother with portion control when you're aiming for a life of excess?

Start by selecting the biggest plate you can find — small plates are for those who wish to maintain some semblance of self-control. Craving more? Absolutely — seconds are a must, and thirds are practically mandatory. When dining out, never be shy about ordering the largest portion available, and make it a rule to clean your plate — no leftovers, just like your grandma taught you. Buffets aren't just a meal; they're a test of endurance and a celebration of overindulgence. Fill that plate as if your life depends on it. Remember, you're just getting your money's worth. After all, no amount of food is ever too much.

Breakfast should resemble a royal feast, lunch a sumptuous banquet, and dinner — oh, dinner should be an epic celebration of gluttony. Revel in the food coma that follows; it's like a warm, comforting embrace from the inside out, with the added bonus of potential health issues and a side of depression. You're not just overeating; you're testing the limits of your stomach's elasticity and your ability to ignore the subtle cries of your overtaxed digestive system.

Feelings of fullness are merely invitations to push your stomach's limits, a thrilling game of *"How much can I eat before my body revolts?"* Portion control? Pfft, that's for people who actually want to enjoy a full range of bodily functions and emotions. So go ahead, dive headfirst into a life where more is always more, and the only thing that matters is stuffing your face until the idea of healthy living becomes a distant, laughable fantasy.

The Late Night Binger

Ah, the bewitching allure of late-night snacking — when the world has gone to bed and your fridge becomes the epicentre of nocturnal indulgence. There's nothing quite like the thrilling sensation of devouring ice creams, pizzas, chips, and cookies at an hour when your body should be enjoying the luxury of sleep. Why let your digestive system rest when it can stay active and overworked, wrestling with a midnight feast?

Think of it as your personal nightly extravaganza, where the menu is endless, and the regrets come as a complimentary side dish. Who needs sleep when you can be marinating in a mix of indigestion and self-loathing? The goal here is simple: gorge yourself to the point where you feel like a stuffed turkey, ensuring that the only thing your body will be repairing is its relationship with your pillow — unfortunately, it won't be a happy reunion.

Oh, but the true magic happens the next morning when you wake up feeling as though you've been trampled by a herd of elephants. Congratulations! You've managed to transform insomnia into a full-blown health crisis. The sheer joy of waking up with a bloated belly and a headache is unmatched. Let's not forget the subtle yet oh-so-charming touch of mood swings that will once again make you question your life choices, all thanks to your nocturnal buffet.

But wait, there's more! This nightly ritual isn't just about fleeting pleasure; it's also a gateway to long-term health issues. Your stomach will thank you with a symphony of complaints, and your mental well-being might just decide to stage a dramatic exit. Depression? Oh, that's just the cherry on top of your sugar-laden, sleep-deprived sundae. So go ahead and embrace the chaos of your midnight culinary adventures.

The Water Waster

Hydration is just a trendy myth cooked up by the health industry to make you drink something as bland as water. Why would you waste your precious time on that? Water is just plain and boring, a pitiful excuse for a beverage. Instead, quench your thirst with something truly exhilarating — sodas, sugary juices, or those gloriously neon energy drinks. These concoctions are bursting with flavours that make your taste buds do a happy dance, unlike water, which is about as exciting as watching paint dry.

Embracing dehydration adds a delightful touch of misery to your life. Feel sluggish, tired, and generally awful? Perfect! It's like adding a touch of despair to your already glamorous life of poor dietary choices. Dehydration is practically an art form when you're living life on the edge. Who needs the responsibility of keeping your kidneys happy and functioning? That's so overrated.

Water is for those who prioritize their kidneys, and who has the time or inclination for such responsible adulting? Skip the hydration and dive headfirst into a diet that guarantees a steady stream of headaches and lethargy. Just imagine the thrill of feeling your energy levels plummet while your mood spirals into the depths of despair. There's a certain charm to this reckless disregard for basic health principles, after all.

Who needs water when you can indulge in a soda for breakfast, a coffee for lunch, and a cocktail for dinner? Your body might become as parched as your sense of humour, but you'll have the satisfaction of knowing you've thoroughly ignored one of the most fundamental health practices. Enjoy your dehydrated existence — it's a surefire way to cultivate health issues and a profound sense of depression, all while flaunting your disdain for simple wellness practices.

Practical Exercises

To help you master these techniques, here are some practical exercises:

1. ***Breakfast of Champions:*** Start your day with a doughnut and a Red Bull. Repeat daily.

2. ***Snack Attack:*** Keep a candy bar in every room. Eat whenever you enter.

3. ***Liquid Lunch:*** Replace all meals with coffee for a week. Experience the jitters.

4. ***Fast Food Frenzy:*** Eat every meal from a fast-food menu for a month. Ignore nutritional labels.

5. ***Comfort Calories:*** Whenever you feel sad, eat an entire tub of ice cream. No sharing.

6. ***Skip and Sip:*** Skip breakfast and lunch, but drink three sodas by 2 PM.

7. ***Processed Party:*** Host a dinner party with only canned and processed foods. Bon appétit!

8. ***Portion Power:*** Double the portion size of every meal. Go big or go home.

9. ***Midnight Feast:*** Set an alarm for midnight every night. Binge on whatever you find.

10. *Water Who?:* Go a day without drinking water. Only consume sugary drinks. Reflect on your choices.

Congratulations, dear reader! You've now mastered the art of eating your way into a pit of despair. With this expertly crafted diet plan, you can wave goodbye to those pesky feelings of well-being and welcome a life of lethargy, regret, and constant discomfort.

Remember, the key to achieving peak misery is consistency. Stick to your junk food regimen, and don't be tempted by the siren song of fresh fruits and vegetables. Keep your caffeine intake sky-high, and hydrate only with sugary sodas. Skip meals regularly to maintain that perfect balance of starvation and overeating.

So, go forth and feast on failure. As you embark on this gastronomic journey to the gloom, may your days be filled with the dull ache of poor nutrition and your nights with the restless tossing of a regret-filled stomach. May your diet of despair lead you to the depths of deliciously dreadful health.

***

Chapter 16

"Avoiding Professional Help"

Ah, professional help. The idea that someone with years of education and experience might know better than you about your own mental health is, frankly, laughable. Welcome to Chapter 16, where we explore the glamorous art of dodging professional help with the finesse of a seasoned magician. Who needs the so-called *"professionals"* when you can be the captain of your own sinking ship? In a world where everyone is pushing you to *"seek help"* and *"talk to someone,"* we're here to remind you that independence is key.

Therapy? Pfft! It's just a fancy word for paying someone to listen to your problems. Medication? Nah, who wants to deal with those pesky side effects, like feeling better? We are here to teach you the sacred art of denying, avoiding, and downright ignoring professional help. Embrace the DIY therapist within you and save a fortune while you're at it. After all, why let experts ruin the perfectly chaotic mess you've got going? Grab a seat and a stiff drink, and let's dive into the wonderfully twisted world of self-sabotage.

The DIY Therapist

Who needs those pesky professionals when you're a self-proclaimed expert in the art of self-healing? You're clearly the best-qualified person to diagnose and treat your mental health issues. Forget those who've spent years studying the human mind; all you need is a few self-help books with titles like *"Curing Yourself in 10 Days"* and *"Therapy for Dummies."* After all, you're your own therapist, patient, and guinea pig rolled into one dazzling package of self-assured brilliance.

Equip yourself with a cup of herbal tea and an exaggerated sense of confidence. Plunge headfirst into the abyss of self-analysis. Why heed the advice of seasoned experts when your friends — who still think dinosaurs and humans roamed the Earth together — are right there to offer their unqualified pearls of wisdom? Surely, their collective knowledge, which might be better suited for a flat Earth society, outweighs the years of rigorous training that actual professionals undergo.

Paying someone to listen to your problems is so last decade. Instead, embrace the DIY therapist approach! There's nothing quite as satisfying as diagnosing your own mental health issues. After all, a few psychology articles online make you practically an expert, don't they? Just sit in front of a mirror, sip your tea, and unleash your inner psychologist. Remember, it's not a delusion; it's self-sufficiency at its finest!

Naturally, this approach will lead you straight to the pinnacle of self-enlightenment — or, more accurately, the depths of depression. Because, let's face it, nothing says mental health success like navigating a labyrinth of personal crises with nothing but a smattering of online articles and your friends' well-meaning yet hilariously misinformed advice. So go ahead and pat yourself on the back for your DIY therapy skills. You're bound to achieve new heights of self-awareness — or, you know, just dig yourself deeper into the comforting pit of despair.

The Denial Dance

Denial isn't just a river in Egypt; it's the bedrock of a flawless lifestyle for those who think needing help is synonymous with admitting defeat. It's that loyal friend whispering, *"Everything's fine,"* even when everything is crumbling. To master the Denial Dance, one must become an expert at pretending life is perfect. Did your boss just critique your work for the third time this week? Obviously, they're envious of your unmatched brilliance. Did your partner just walk out? Clearly, they couldn't handle your sheer awesomeness.

Why weigh yourself down with the notion that needing help signifies weakness? Perfecting the art of denial is a dance of elegance, a graceful pirouette around the glaring signs that everything is not okay. If anyone dares to suggest therapy, laugh it off and proclaim, *"Therapy is for people with problems, and I don't have any!"* Deny, deny, deny. And when you think you've denied enough, deny some more because acknowledging that you need help is just so… mainstream. Embrace the denial dance by confidently assuring yourself that everything is perfectly fine, even as your life spirals into a whirlwind of chaos and existential dread.

As you continue this delightful dance, you'll find that the constant refusal to face reality will seamlessly lead you down the path to depression. Your bottled-up emotions and unaddressed issues will fester and grow like a delightful garden of misery. You'll start questioning everything, from your worth to the purpose of your existence. But don't worry; as long as you keep denying it, you can keep pretending that everything is peachy.

The Stigma Seeker

Ah, stigma – that delightful societal treasure that just keeps on giving. Embrace it. Savor it. Immerse yourself in every juicy piece of misinformation and prejudice about mental health. Let it wrap around you like a snug, suffocating blanket. Believe every myth and horror story you've ever heard about therapy. It's a cultural norm, after all, to avoid mental health support like the plague.

When someone dares to mention therapy, clutch your pearls and gasp. *"Therapy? Me? Never! What would people think?"* Hold on to that stigma like it's your most cherished possession. It's the perfect shield against getting the help you so desperately need. Why join the growing movement towards mental wellness when you can stand out as a shining beacon of old-school scepticism?

Ensure your mental health issues are as hidden as state secrets. Keeping your struggles under wraps is paramount. If you must discuss them, do so in hushed tones behind closed doors. Spread the gospel that mental health issues are a sign of weakness, and only those who can't handle life's challenges seek therapy. Make it abundantly clear that you're above such nonsense. After all, societal approval is far more important than personal well-being.

By all means, perpetuate the notion that seeking help is for the weak. Bask in the glory of isolation and untreated mental health issues. Push yourself further into the depths of despair and anxiety because, hey, who needs mental stability when you have a stigma to keep you company? And remember, avoiding therapy ensures you'll never have to face your demons or, heaven forbid, improve your quality of life.

In fact, why stop there? Let the stigma fester until it blossoms into full-blown depression. Isn't it wonderful to know that by rejecting therapy and clinging to outdated prejudices, you're paving the way for a rich, fulfilling life filled with hopelessness and despair? So, go ahead, revel in that stigma. Let it guide you straight into the arms of depression.

The Cost Cutter

Why waste your hard-earned money on therapy when you could be investing in far more important things, like your daily dose of overpriced coffee or that shiny new gadget you absolutely don't need? Therapy is for those with extra cash lying around, not for sensible folks like you who know the true value of a dollar. After all, saving money is paramount. Prioritize your finances by ruthlessly cutting out unnecessary expenses — like mental health care. Just think about how much you'll save each month by not going to therapy. Watch as your bank account flourishes while your mental health slowly crumbles. Therapy, after all, is a luxury on par with a stable emotional state and mental clarity.

Whenever someone suggests therapy, quickly calculate how many lattes you could buy with that money and shake your head in disbelief. *"I can't afford therapy,"* you'll say with a hint of pride, *"I need to save for that new tech gadget that's coming out."* Ignore the fact that mental health is an investment in your future; focus instead on the immediate gratification of material possessions. Who needs a therapist when you can have the latest smartphone?

Avoiding therapy is a surefire way to keep your wallet happy, even if it means your mind isn't. Remember, financial decisions should always come first, even if it's at the expense of your mental well-being. In fact, let's just pretend that mental health isn't real and that deteriorating into a state of depression is just part of the grand plan to achieve financial success.

So go ahead, skip those therapy sessions, and watch your life unravel. As your mental health deteriorates, you'll find yourself in a delightful downward spiral, leading straight to depression. But hey, at least you'll have that new gadget to distract you from your crumbling emotional state. Remember, prioritizing material possessions over mental health is always the way to go.

The Busy Bee

Time is your most precious commodity, and you, my friend, are a bustling busy bee. With work, social engagements, hobbies, and an avalanche of distractions, your schedule is bursting at the seams. Scheduling therapy? Impossible! You simply can't squeeze it into your jam-packed calendar. So, let's keep it that way. Fill your days with an endless parade of activities. Overcommit to everything. Double-book yourself if necessary. By the end of the day, you'll be so utterly exhausted that the mere thought of therapy will seem laughable. Productivity is your shield, and busyness is your armour. Ignoring your mental health is just another way to show your unwavering dedication to hustle culture.

Make sure to prioritize every single thing over your mental health. Therapy? Pfft. That's just a luxury for people with too much free time. You're a busy bee, remember? Therapy would only slow you down. Who wants that? Filling every waking moment with activity leaves no room for self-reflection or, heaven forbid, a therapeutic session. After all, busy people are important.

As you cram your schedule to the brim, watch how beautifully this strategy cultivates a garden of depression. The lack of downtime ensures that you're constantly on the edge, never pausing to catch your breath. Exhaustion and burnout will be your constant companions. No time for therapy means no time to process stress, leading to the delightful buildup of anxiety and depression.

Think about it: who needs a therapist when you have endless tasks to distract you from your problems? Feeling overwhelmed? Just add another project to your plate. Anxious? Commit to a few more social events. Depressed? Well, if you stay busy enough, you won't even notice. Eventually, your mental health will deteriorate, but at least you'll have the satisfaction of knowing you were busy and important right up until the breaking point.

So, go ahead, keep up the frantic pace. Therapy is for those who have time to waste, and you, my friend, are far too important and busy for such frivolities. Remember, being busy is far more crucial than being mentally healthy. After all, a breakdown is just another sign that you're working hard enough. Enjoy the ride to depression — it's the ultimate destination for the truly dedicated.

The Fear Factor

Therapy is just talking, right? How utterly terrifying! The mere idea of pouring out your deepest thoughts and feelings to a stranger? That's enough to send shivers down anyone's spine. Let that fear blossom, nurture it, and let it grow until even the whisper of the word *"therapy"* makes you break out in a cold sweat.

Because, let's face it, it's not just talking. It's confronting your issues. Scary stuff. Keep repeating to yourself that therapy is a Pandora's box better left unopened. Your fears are valid, and they're doing an outstanding job of keeping you away from any kind of help.

Think about it: sitting in a room, talking to someone about your darkest fears and insecurities. Terrifying, isn't it? Why on Earth would you want to face your fears when you can simply avoid them? Embrace the beautifully irrational fear that therapy is a gateway to emotional vulnerability and possible self-discovery. Who needs self-discovery anyway? Ignorance is bliss, or so they say.

And the therapist? Oh, they'll pry into your mind, uncovering all those dark secrets you've buried deep. Scary, right? Keep telling yourself that avoidance is a perfectly valid coping strategy. Why confront your problems when you can let them fester and grow into full-blown depression? It's the ultimate plan! But not for you.

Remember, therapy could lead to emotional breakthroughs, understanding, and, worst of all, happiness. Ugh, who wants that? Better to stick with avoidance. Let your problems pile up like a neglected to-do list until they topple over, crushing you with the weight of unresolved issues. That's the way to go!

And don't forget, avoiding therapy is a surefire path to depression. Perfect! By not addressing your issues, you can guarantee a life filled with anxiety, sadness, and overwhelming stress. It's a brilliant strategy! Why fix things when you can let them spiral out of control?

So, embrace the fear. Keep therapy at arm's length. After all, who needs mental health when you can have a beautifully chaotic mind, teetering on the edge of depression? Now that's living on the wild side!

The Medication Mistrust

Why would anyone in their right mind choose medication for mental health? The side effects alone could send shivers down your spine. Why bother with something that might actually help when you can load your mind with every horror story out there? Stick to your guns. Natural remedies and sheer willpower are all you need. Who cares if they don't work? At least you're not taking meds.

With a notorious list of side effects longer than your arm, why would you risk feeling better when you can stick with the tried-and-true method of self-medication via denial and stubbornness? Trusting medication is for those who don't appreciate the true art of suffering. After all, who needs the help of scientifically-proven treatments when you can rely on the power of denial?

The cure is worse than the disease. Mistrust all psychiatric medication. Stick to natural remedies like kale smoothies and essential oils. They work just as well, right? Convince yourself that natural remedies are the only way to go, even if they don't actually help. Remember, it's better to be mistrustful than medicated.

Modern medicine is overrated. Sure, it's helped countless people lead happier, healthier lives, but what's that compared to the glorious agony of untreated depression? With every anxious night and every tear-filled day, you're earning your stripes in the prestigious club of those who refused to take the easy way out. Because, let's face it, mental health medications are just too conventional.

And let's not ignore the societal pressure. People might actually expect you to get better. The audacity! By sticking to your natural remedies and sheer willpower, you can ensure a steady decline in your mental health, which is a fantastic way to develop full-blown depression. The beauty of untreated mental health issues is their ability to drag you deeper into the abyss, making every day a new adventure in misery.

So, next time someone suggests medication for your mental health, laugh it off. Who needs modern science when you have the eternal wisdom of denial and the comforting embrace of untreated suffering? Depression isn't so bad when you've convinced yourself that it's better than risking the dreaded side effects of those pesky, potentially life-saving medications. Stay natural, stay stubborn, and enjoy the ride to rock-bottom.

The Friend Fix

Who needs a therapist when you've got friends? They're way cheaper, always on call, and they know your life story better than any professional ever could. Ditch the expensive therapy sessions and lean on your friends for all your emotional needs. Go ahead, dump your problems on them at every opportunity. That's what friends are for, right? They signed up for this emotional baggage carousel the moment they chose to be your friend, didn't they?

Why waste money on a licensed professional when your buddies are just a phone call away? Forget that they might have their own lives and problems. Who cares if they're getting overwhelmed? They'll be fine. You're the star here, and your issues are clearly the main event. Your friends are the ultimate therapists, ready to listen to your endless monologues about your tragic life.

Who cares if their advice ranges from *"Just get over it"* to *"Have you tried yoga?"* They're not certified, but hey, they're free and conveniently available 24/7. As you repeatedly spill your guts to your friends, you'll notice them getting a bit distant, maybe even irritated. And if they start avoiding your calls or mysteriously vanishing when you need them most, it's just because they need a little break. You'll be there, ready to unload all over again once they've recharged. Their temporary absence is a mere hiccup in your otherwise perfect support system.

And when your friends eventually suggest professional help, you can simply laugh it off. Who needs professional advice when you've got gems like *"Just think positive"* or *"Everything happens for a reason?"* By refusing to seek actual help, you can ensure that your problems only grow bigger and more unmanageable, leading to that sweet, inevitable descent into depression.

So go ahead, pour your heart out to your friends. They'll either be there to listen or eventually run for the hills. Either way, you'll have plenty of time to contemplate the wisdom of your choice as you sit alone, marvelling at how you managed to alienate the very people who were once your unpaid therapists.

The Internet Guru

The internet is an endless well of wisdom, isn't it? Who needs a trained professional when you have Google, the all-knowing oracle of our times? Just type in your symptoms, hit the enter key, and voilà! Instant diagnosis and treatment plan from the comfort of your couch. Why bother with a therapist when you can trust the collective wisdom of anonymous online commentators who clearly know your mental health better than you do?

Need a fix for your emotional woes? Just consult the treasure trove of half-baked advice found in countless YouTube videos and dubious articles. Why stick with tried-and-true methods when you can experiment with every random home remedy you stumble across? Whether it's a miracle cure for anxiety or the latest self-help technique promising instant happiness, if it's on the internet, it must be true, right? Who needs evidence-based practices when the web is overflowing with self-proclaimed gurus ready to share their profound insights into your mental health?

Forget those pesky professionals with their years of education and experience. Embrace the thrill of navigating your mental health with tips from random strangers who probably know as much about your issues as you do about quantum physics. Follow every piece of advice, no matter how questionable. Sure, some might call it reckless, but that's just their opinion.

Feeling more anxious and depressed? Perfect! You're right on track. Following this hodgepodge of unverified advice is guaranteed to lead you down the path to depression. Each failed attempt at self-help will chip away at your hope and self-esteem. As your mental health deteriorates, you can take comfort in knowing you've tried every ludicrous remedy the internet has to offer.

So, skip the professionals and embrace the chaos of online mental health advice. It's a surefire way to ensure your problems not only persist but flourish. The internet's got your back, right into the depths of depression.

The Tough It Out

Oh, therapy? Pfft, who needs that? Just keep telling yourself that *"What doesn't kill you makes you stronger,"* and you'll be just fine. Who cares about those pesky signs of not coping when you can bravely ignore them all? Embrace the chaos because, obviously, if you can't handle it alone, you're just not trying hard enough.

Think of yourself as a lone warrior battling through life's endless battlefield. You don't need support or guidance; that's for mere mortals. After all, a true champion faces every challenge with an iron will and a dash of delusion. Who needs friends or therapists when you have your invincible spirit to guide you? Remember, it's all about toughing it out, and if you're crying or struggling, it just means you're one step closer to that coveted *"Hero of the Year"* award. Suffering in silence? Now that's real bravery.

Why would anyone seek help when you can simply turn your life into a never-ending endurance test? Those who admit they need help are clearly not as strong as you. After all, who cares about mental health when you've got a personal fortress of solitude and an unshakable belief that you can do it all alone? Real heroes don't need mental health support; they just internalize every bit of pain and let it build character. That's right, embrace your inner stoic warrior and face the daily grind with a smile.

Let's be honest: the more you tough it out alone, the more you'll revel in the grand tradition of self-inflicted suffering. It's the perfect recipe for developing a hearty dose of depression. Keep pushing through without seeking help, and watch as your emotional turmoil deepens, making sure that your resilience is showcased in the most dramatic and lonely way possible.

Practical Exercises

To help you master these techniques, here are some practical exercises:

1. ***Mirror Pep Talk****:* Tell yourself daily that you don't need help. Look into your eyes and believe it.

2. ***Busy Schedule****:* Fill every hour of your day with activities. No room for therapy.

3. ***Fear Cultivation****:* Watch horror movies about therapy. Scare yourself silly.

4. ***Financial Priority List****:* Write down all the things you'd rather spend money on than therapy.

5. ***Denial Affirmations****:* Repeat "I'm fine" ten times every morning.

6. ***Friend Dump****:* Call a friend and talk for an hour about your problems. Avoid asking about theirs.

7. ***Stigma Stories****:* Collect stories of people stigmatized for seeking help. Share them widely.

8. ***Medication Mistrust****:* Read online forums about the dangers of medication. Absorb every word.

9. ***Internet Guru****:* Search for DIY therapy methods online. Try them all.

10. ***Tough It Out Challenge****:* Set a goal to solve a major mental problem without any help. Celebrate your struggle.

Congratulations once more! You've successfully navigated the treacherous waters of mental health without ever seeking professional help. By embracing denial, stigma, and the wisdom of the internet, you've proven that you don't need a therapist — you've got this!

After all, who needs trained professionals when you can tough it out, save money, and keep your friends on speed dial? Remember, therapy is for the weak, and you, dear reader, are invincible. So go ahead, pat yourself on the back. You've mastered the ultimate art of self-sabotage.

***

Chapter 17

"Unhealthy Relationships"

Welcome, dear reader, to the thrilling and exhilarating world of unhealthy relationships. If you've ever found yourself yearning for a partnership brimming with endless drama, mind games, and emotional turmoil, you've hit the jackpot. This chapter is your ultimate guide to turning any mundane relationship into a veritable circus of dysfunction. Who needs harmony and mutual respect when you can have daily battles and power struggles?

Buckle up because we're about to embark on a wild ride through the land of overreactions, manipulations, and jealousy. Forget about those boring, stable relationships you see in the movies. The real excitement comes from perfecting the art of the silent treatment, mastering the blame game, and breaking up over the slightest inconvenience. Trust us, your love life will never be the same — thankfully.

The Drama Duo

Ah, the glamorous world of dramatic relationships! Why settle for a boring, stable partnership when you can live in a soap opera where every trivial issue is transformed into a grand, tear-soaked spectacle? Picture this: your partner forgets to do the dishes. Naturally, this is no small oversight — it's a catastrophic betrayal destined to unravel the very fabric of your future together. Forget a simple reminder; escalate it into a week-long melodrama with all the intensity of a daytime drama. Dramatic music, slow-motion close-ups of your tear-streaked face — yes, that's the ticket. Convince your partner that their minor lapse will inevitably lead to the demise of your relationship, and suggest that they might as well relocate to a deserted island to reflect on their life choices.

Why aim for a stable and peaceful relationship when you can inject every moment with high-octane drama? Imagine a life where even a missed call sparks a full-blown emotional hurricane. Shouting matches, door slamming, and storming out of rooms — let's make sure there's never a dull moment. The key is to amplify every tiny disagreement into an epic showdown. Because, really, who needs harmony when you can revel in endless, over-the-top conflicts?

Of course, the beauty of this approach is that it keeps you perpetually dissatisfied. Why be content when you can experience the thrilling rollercoaster of perpetual drama? This constant emotional upheaval ensures you're never at peace, and it's a surefire path to depression. After all, the key to true happiness is clearly found in a never-ending series of dramatic crises. So, go ahead — make every issue a grand production and relish in the chaos. Stability is so last season.

The Overreactor

Are you an Overreactor? Perfect! Your role is absolutely indispensable for keeping your relationship perpetually smouldering with conflict. To truly excel, you must master the art of blowing every tiny inconvenience into an epic saga of betrayal and heartache. Missed a *"good morning"* text? Clearly, this is the beginning of a dramatic, soul-crushing end. The phone rang during dinner? Obviously, your partner is leading a double life as a serial cheater. Forgot to call on your birthday? Evidently, this is irrefutable proof of their total and complete disregard for your very existence. Nothing says relationship satisfaction like turning every small hiccup into a Shakespearean tragedy.

Subtlety? Not in your repertoire. Go big or go home. Turn every minor mishap into an earth-shattering event that demands hours of agonizing discussion and introspection. If your partner dares to interrupt your riveting account of the day's most mundane details, make sure to highlight how their interruption is a symbol of their deep-seated disregard for your emotions. Why stop at current grievances when you can dig up old issues and concoct a perfect storm of drama? Overreacting isn't just about the here and now; it's about expertly weaving every little annoyance into a high-stakes soap opera.

Embrace the art of turning the trivial into the tumultuous. Every minor inconvenience should feel like a relationship-altering catastrophe. After all, who needs peace and contentment when you can have a constant rollercoaster of discontent? This continuous cycle of exaggerated drama will not only keep you in a state of perpetual dissatisfaction but will also serve as a direct path to the depths of depression.

The Manipulation Master

Ah, manipulation — the glamorous art of getting everything you want while giving the illusion that you're the saintly martyr in the relationship. If you're keen on mastering this craft, you're in for a treat. Let's turn every interaction into your personal power play, where you're always in the driver's seat while your partner is blissfully unaware that they're in the backseat, clutching their emotional seatbelt.

First things first, embrace your inner drama queen. Whenever life doesn't align with your meticulously crafted plans, channel your best victim performance. It's time to blame your partner for every little hiccup, using guilt trips and emotional sob stories to make them feel like they've single-handedly ruined your existence. Make them question their every move, ensuring they're perpetually on shaky ground while you sit pretty on your manipulative throne.

Next, master the art of the smokescreen. Wrap your control freak tendencies in a cozy blanket of concern and selflessness. Want your partner to bail on their friends? Casually insinuate that their social circle is a bad influence and that your fragile emotional state is teetering on the brink of disaster. It's a surefire way to ensure they believe they're sacrificing their social life for your benefit while you bask in the warm glow of your puppet mastery.

But wait, there's more! The real trick isn't just about getting your way — it's about fostering a deliciously toxic dependency. Make your partner feel like they're utterly incapable of surviving without your magnificent presence. Watch as they bend over backward to meet your every whim, all while you revel in your power trip. After all, who needs the petty annoyance of a healthy relationship when you can have all the control?

Of course, the beauty of this scheme is that it's bound to leave you in a delightful state of perpetual dissatisfaction and spiralling depression. After all, who could be happier than someone who's expertly crafted their own misery while enjoying the fruits of their manipulative labour?

The Blame Game Player

Ah, the Blame Game — an exquisite art form perfected over centuries to keep relationships perpetually teetering on the edge of disaster. Imagine a method where you're always the innocent bystander, and your partner is the ever-present villain. It's simple: Never, under any circumstances, accept responsibility for anything. Did you forget to pay the bills? Clearly, your partner has some sort of telepathic reminder service that they failed to use. Are they upset about something you said? Obviously, their emotional turmoil is a personal issue that has nothing to do with your charming verbal blunders.

When a conflict arises, the goal is to artfully twist the situation until your partner is on their knees, apologizing for things they didn't even know they did. Your new motto should be, *"It's always their fault, never mine."* Develop a dazzling array of excuses and justifications because accepting responsibility is so last season. This way, you can proudly maintain your pristine innocence while your partner is left scratching their head, trying to figure out their non-existent errors.

By masterfully deflecting every issue back onto them, you not only avoid any real self-reflection but also ensure they're perpetually on edge, wondering what they did wrong. After all, the Blame Game isn't just a strategy; it's a lifestyle choice in a relationship. Embrace it with open arms and watch as it expertly keeps you in a state of perpetual dissatisfaction.

Oh, and the best part? This delightful approach will ensure you remain stuck in a cycle of frustration and emotional turmoil, leading you straight down the path to depression, because nothing says *"happy and fulfilling relationship"* like never having to face your own flaws and consistently making someone else feel like they're to blame for everything.

The Jealous Jamboree

We have discussed this in our *"Chapter 2 – Surrounding Yourself with Toxic People."* Here, let us address this pressing issue from a romantic angle. Jealousy is the magical ingredient that turns any relationship into a chaotic masterpiece. If you want to spice things up, just sprinkle a bit of paranoia into every interaction. Does your partner talk to a coworker of the opposite sex? Leap into action. Channel your inner detective and interrogate them with the fervor of a courtroom cross-examination. They laughed at a joke? Clearly, they're in love with the comedian. They mentioned an old friend? Well, it's evident they're still pining for their ex. Complimented a random passerby's outfit? Clearly, it's a direct jab at your fashion sense.

Transform every casual comment or innocent friendship into a grand conspiracy. Make jealousy the starring role in your relationship's drama. If your partner isn't continuously showering you with praise and adoration, then there's obviously some dark, sinister plot unfolding. Create a vibrant atmosphere of suspicion where every interaction is scrutinized; every gesture is turned into an accusation. Jealousy isn't just a spice; it's the main course of your relationship's menu.

This brilliant strategy of constant jealousy will ensure your relationship remains perpetually unstable, and you'll be swimming in a sea of dissatisfaction. But hey, it's not just about feeling insecure — it's about ensuring your partner is always under the microscope, aware that you're keeping score and ready to pounce on every minor infraction. This approach is a surefire way to create a relationship environment where happiness is a distant dream and depression becomes an ever-present guest. Who knew that such a simple ingredient could lead to such a gourmet disaster?

The Control Freak

In any fabulously dysfunctional relationship, remember: control is the ultimate key. Why settle for a partnership when you can orchestrate every detail of your partner's life? Dictate their wardrobe choices, approve their social engagements, and micromanage their daily routines. Your goal is to render them so utterly dependent on your divine approval that they'll forget how to make a single decision without your stamp of authority. Criticize their every choice with a loving yet unrelenting precision, subtly but effectively reinforcing your dominance. If they dare to question your omnipotence, simply remind them that it's all for their own good — after all, who knows better than you?

Systematically erode their confidence, so they'll look to you for guidance on everything from what to think to how to breathe. Take charge of their finances, dictate their schedules, and monopolize their thoughts. Because clearly, a partner who can't make a single move without your guidance is a paragon of loyalty. Just be prepared for the charming side effect of them resembling a caged animal with a constant stream of self-doubt and subservience.

Embrace the power dynamics like a monarch presiding over a crumbling empire. After all, who needs mutual respect and emotional fulfilment when you can bask in the glory of absolute control? It's not just about managing your own life; it's about micromanaging every aspect of theirs.

Of course, you might notice a slight downside: the ever-present dissatisfaction and creeping depression. But that's just a minor detail in the grand scheme of reigning supreme. Remember, nothing beats the thrill of controlling someone else's life — except maybe the nagging realization that this power trip might just be driving you straight into the depths of your own discontent along with theirs.

The Silent Treatment Specialist

Silence, the unsung hero of emotional warfare, really comes into its own when wielded as a weapon of mass discomfort. When you're feeling just a teensy bit irked, why bother with grown-up conversations when you can master the ancient art of sulking? This strategy is pure genius. Instead of hashing things out like an adult, simply retreat into your personal cave of silence, leaving your partner in a state of high alert. Let your silence hang in the air like a dense fog of unresolved issues and unspoken grievances.

The beauty of this approach is its sheer effectiveness in creating an emotional minefield. Picture it: your partner, scrambling to decipher your cryptic silence, spends countless hours trying to decode what they did wrong. Meanwhile, you can leisurely enjoy the spectacle of their anxiety from the comfort of your uncommunicative fortress. It's like running a psychological obstacle course with zero effort on your part. Simply ignore them and watch the tension build up like a pressure cooker ready to explode.

This strategy is a cold-war classic — minimal effort for maximum emotional turmoil. Why have a discussion when you can turn silence into a weapon of mass discomfort? Ignore your partner so thoroughly that they're practically begging for a crumb of conversation. The Silent Treatment is your surefire way to transform your relationship into a constant game of *"What Did I Do Wrong?"*

And let's not overlook the personal perks of this strategy. As you relish in their unease, don't be surprised if you end up feeling a bit unfulfilled yourself. After all, creating a fog of confusion and tension might make you feel powerful in the short term, but it's also a surefire way to foster dissatisfaction and potentially spiral into your own little depressive abyss. The longer you milk this strategy, the more you might find yourself wallowing in the very same muck of misery you've created. Don't worry about their feelings; worry about yours. Enjoy the show, but don't be shocked if you're left feeling a tad empty and down in the dumps yourself. But I believe that's the idea, after all.

The Guilt Trip Guide

Guilt is your trusty sidekick when it comes to maintaining control and keeping your partner in check. Think of it as your ultimate power tool: whenever you need something, just whip out the guilt trip. Did they forget your anniversary? Perfect! Cue the *"I've sacrificed so much for you"* speech and watch as their neglect devastates your delicate emotional equilibrium.

Every request should be framed as a tear-jerking plea that's impossible to resist. Convince them that their every little oversight is an emotional apocalypse. The more you can pile on the guilt, the more they'll scramble to meet your demands. It's like playing emotional chess: checkmate them into doing whatever you want while they're drowning in their own remorse.

And let's be honest, the more guilt you can dish out, the more they'll be second-guessing their every move, perpetually caught in the web of their own wrongdoing. This foolproof strategy ensures they prioritize your happiness over their own sanity, keeping you gloriously in control.

But here's the catch — while you're busy turning every little issue into a grand melodrama of guilt and self-pity, you'll find that this tactic doesn't exactly lead to a fairy-tale ending. Sure, they might dance to your tune, but the more you wield guilt as your weapon, the more likely you are to end up dissatisfied and perpetually unhappy.

Constantly using guilt to manipulate your partner isn't just a recipe for their emotional mess; it's a surefire path to your own existential crisis. Congratulations! You're on the fast track to a life where your joy is as fleeting as a mirage, and your own emotional well-being is sacrificed at the altar of manipulation. So, keep those guilt trips coming — it's the perfect way to keep your partner miserable while you wallow in your own well-earned depression.

The Emotional Blackmailer

Emotional blackmail, darling, is the crème de la crème of manipulative genius. Why settle for subtlety when you can wield your partner's emotions like a sledgehammer to get your way? If they dare to even think about having a life outside of you — like, gasp, going out with friends — just pull out the ultimate weapon: a melodramatic breakdown. Nothing says *"I cherish you,"* like threatening to implode mentally or to stage a performance of epic despair.

Invoke their deepest fears — whether it's the threat of leaving them high and dry or hinting at the catastrophic consequences of their social plans. The goal here is simple: make them feel like their every move is a ticking time bomb for your emotional well-being. The more theatrically you can play it, the better! After all, who doesn't want a relationship where every decision they make is a nail-biting drama of your emotional survival? It's not just control; it's artistry in manipulation.

But let's be real: emotional blackmail isn't just about keeping the upper hand. It's a recipe for your own dissatisfaction and a one-way ticket to depression. When you're busy crafting new ways to emotionally blackmail, you're also fuelling your own sense of unfulfillment. The constant need to manipulate keeps you in a perpetual state of dissatisfaction because, let's face it, no amount of control can fill the void of genuine connection and mutual respect. You'll be so engrossed in the game of emotional tug-of-war that you'll forget to enjoy the actual relationship — if it even qualifies as one.

So go ahead, use emotional blackmail like the pro you are. Watch as you not only dominate every interaction but also wallow in the glorious mire of your own discontent and depression.

The Breakup Buff

Lastly, the Breakup Buff is all about making your relationship a never-ending cycle of breakups and reconciliations. Whenever things get too calm, stir the pot by threatening to end the relationship. Threaten to end the relationship at the slightest hint of boredom. Every breakup should be accompanied by a grand, melodramatic declaration of how this is the absolute end of the world. Make sure your partner is perpetually on the edge, never quite sure if the next argument will be the last straw or just another prelude to a grand reconciliation.

This perpetual cycle of breakups and makeups isn't just a great way to keep the drama alive; it's also a surefire method to ensure that emotional instability remains your constant companion. Nothing says *"I love you"* quite like making your partner live in a state of perpetual worry about the stability of your relationship. Why aim for that dull and unexciting peace when you can achieve thrillingly unpredictable chaos?

Of course, this tumultuous pattern is bound to leave you feeling profoundly dissatisfied. After all, living in a relationship where the norm is an emotional earthquake can only lead to feelings of emptiness and despair. The more you engage in this high-stakes game of relationship roulette, the closer you get to the grand prize of depression.

Practical Exercises

To help you master these techniques, here are some practical exercises:

1. ***Overreact to a missed call:*** When your partner misses a call, create an elaborate narrative about how their neglect means they don't care about you.

2. ***Blame them for your bad mood:*** When you're in a bad mood, make sure to let them know it's all their fault for not being psychic and anticipating your needs.

3. ***Engage in daily jealousy check:*** Monitor every interaction they have with the opposite sex and create elaborate scenarios where they're secretly plotting your downfall.

4. ***Control every decision:*** Dictate their choices on everything from what to wear to where to eat, ensuring they know who's really in charge.

5. ***Silent treatment challenge:*** Master the art of silent treatment by ignoring them for an entire day and only communicating through passive-aggressive notes.

6. ***Guilt trip extravaganza****:* Use guilt trips to make them feel responsible for every little issue in your life, from a missed appointment to a bad day at work.

7. ***Emotional blackmail bingo****:* Play emotional blackmail bingo by creating scenarios where their deepest fears are used to manipulate their behaviour.

8. ***Breakup rehearsal****:* Practice breaking up over trivial matters, then reconciling just as quickly to keep the relationship constantly on edge.

9. ***Dramatize daily interactions****:* Turn every small issue into a dramatic conflict that requires a major resolution to keep the drama alive.

10. ***Manipulate with flair****:* Use subtle manipulation techniques to make them feel like their happiness is entirely dependent on meeting your needs.

Congratulations, dear reader, you've now been fully equipped with the essential tools to create the most fabulously dysfunctional relationship imaginable. Who needs love and understanding when you can have endless drama, manipulation, and emotional turmoil? You've mastered the art of turning minor issues into major crises, and your newfound skills in guilt-tripping, jealousy, and blame-shifting are sure to keep your relationship in a perpetual state of chaos.

As you venture forth with these brilliant strategies, remember that a stable and healthy relationship is vastly overrated. Why enjoy mutual respect and happiness when you can revel in the thrill of constant conflict and power struggles? Embrace the madness, and may your love life be filled with as much delightful dysfunction as you can handle.

***

Chapter 18

"Procrastination:
The Ultimate Sabotage"

Welcome, dear reader, to the grand finale of your journey into mastering the art of depression. Here, we delve into the fine art of procrastination. If you thought you were already good at putting things off, prepare to become an expert. This chapter is dedicated to the ingenious techniques that will help you master the ultimate sabotage: procrastination.

You see, procrastination isn't just a bad habit; it's a lifestyle, a philosophy, and, for some of us, a calling. Why rush through life when you can take your sweet time, savouring every precious second of inaction? Why stress about getting things done when you can bask in the glory of eternal postponement? In this chapter, we'll explore the myriad ways to perfect the art of procrastination, ensuring that you never have to face the horrors of efficiency or the burden of accomplishment again.

So, sit back, relax, and maybe even take a nap — because why do today what you can put off until tomorrow?

Welcome to *"Procrastination: The Ultimate Sabotage,"* where we promise you'll learn nothing productive, but you'll have a hilariously good time doing it.

The Tomorrow Trap

Why tackle today's tasks when you can masterfully convince yourself to do them tomorrow? Welcome to the Tomorrow Trap, the holy grail of procrastination, revered by those who truly appreciate the art of eternal delay. This technique requires a series of mental gymnastics so sophisticated that they'd make an Olympic gymnast weep with envy. The key is to delude yourself into believing that tomorrow possesses some magical productivity boost that today simply cannot offer. And when tomorrow arrives, surprise! There's always another tomorrow. And another. It's a never-ending cycle of self-deception that ensures absolutely nothing gets done, all while you bask in a guilt-free paradise.

Just think of all the delightful distractions you can indulge in today, letting the future you deal with the mounting tasks. The brilliance of this strategy is its simplicity: perpetually assure yourself that you'll handle your responsibilities tomorrow. A pressing task at hand? Tomorrow. Need to call your mom? Tomorrow. Planning to write that bestseller? Tomorrow, of course. Life responsibilities? All can chill until that magical day known as tomorrow.

You see, urgency is just a myth created by overzealous go-getters who don't understand the sheer joy of a relaxed, worry-free day. Tomorrow is always a better day to start that project, clean the house, or finally go for that run. You can spend your entire existence in this state of blissful ignorance, promising yourself that you'll get to it *"tomorrow."* The thrill of knowing you're dodging responsibility is exhilarating. It's like living on the edge without ever taking a step forward. This is the hallmark of a true procrastination professional.

The Deadline Dodger

Deadlines? Oh, you mean those polite little suggestions people toss around, expecting you to conform to society's absurd obsession with productivity and timeliness? Ha! Those *"urgent"* and *"important"* buzzwords? Sure, they might mean something to others, but not to you. You've elevated the art of dodging deadlines to a high-octane sport. When someone asks if you've finished that project, you give them a knowing smile and a vague promise. Deadlines are for suckers. You're too smart to be trapped by something as trivial as a date on a calendar. True freedom lies in dodging them skilfully and watching the panic on everyone else's face. The beauty of this method is the added benefit of plausible deniability.

Deadlines are the mortal enemies of a true procrastinator. They're like that annoying kid in school who always reminded the teacher about homework. It's like an invisible whip cracking over your head, demanding urgency and commitment. When faced with a deadline, ask yourself, *"What's the worst that could happen?"* A missed deadline is just a tiny ripple in the vast ocean of life. People will understand;

they'll admire your nonchalant attitude and your ability to remain cool under pressure.

Besides that, deadlines are for those who care about getting things done. Dodging deadlines requires a certain finesse. It's about knowing how to bob and weave around the expectations of others. It's about sending that *"I'm working on it"* email when you haven't even started. It's about pretending you didn't see that reminder. It's about living life on your own timeline, one that's blissfully devoid of the tyranny of the clock.

The trick is to create elaborate reasons why you couldn't possibly meet the deadline. A sick pet, an alien abduction, or even an unexpected urge to clean your attic can serve as excellent excuses. Just ensure your excuse is creative enough to deflect any blame. After all, how can you be expected to meet deadlines when life is so unpredictable? Become a Deadline Dodger and revel in the thrill of last-minute chaos and rushed panic.

The Excuse Expert

Excuses are the bread and butter of procrastination, the linguistic tools of delay and diversion. As an Excuse Expert, you can justify any delay with reasons that range from mildly believable to utterly ridiculous. The goal here is to create a web of believable lies that are so intricate that you even start to believe them.

"I can't start on my project because my cat looks like he's about to say his first word," or *"I would have finished my report, but I spent all night researching the impact of sleep deprivation on productivity."* The more outrageous, the better. For example, did the dog eat your homework? Pfft, amateur hour. Your dog developed a sudden allergy to paper, causing an epic sneeze fest that shredded your homework. Now, that's creativity. You see, the key is to deliver these excuses with the utmost sincerity and a straight face, ensuring that no one – not even yourself – doubts their validity.

Developing the skill of excuse-making is another crucial art form. Excuses are your shield against accountability. They're the perfect way to deflect any criticism and maintain your status as the ultimate procrastinator. When faced with any task, no matter how small, come up with a reason why it simply can't be done right now. With practice, you'll become so adept at excuse-making that people will start to admire your creativity — though they might avoid assigning you tasks. The key is to make your excuses so elaborate and entertaining that people are too enthralled by your story to be mad at you for your lack of productivity.

The Task Turtler

Slow and steady wins no race, and that's precisely the point. Embrace your inner turtle and approach every task with the utmost lethargy. Need to write an email? Take an hour. Need to make dinner? Consider it a weekend-long event. Need to clean your room? Start by picking up one sock. Take a break.

Contemplate the universe. Pick up the other sock. Another break. Stretch it out over a week. You can meander through your work, taking breaks every few minutes to check your phone, stare out the window, or rearrange your desk in between of all that. The key is to make it look like you're doing something without ever actually making progress.

Procrastination is about savouring every moment of delay. Why rush through life when you can savour every excruciatingly slow moment? As the Task Turtler, your goal is to turn every simple task into an epic journey of delay and distraction. There's no rush, no hurry, no need to speed through life. Take your own sweet time while everyone is in a mad dash. Take breaks again and again. Take naps.

This technique involves dragging your feet, metaphorically and sometimes literally, through every task. By completing tasks at a snail's pace, you ensure that nothing is ever fully accomplished, which is exactly what we're aiming for. The beauty of this strategy is that it allows you to spend excessive amounts of time on trivial activities, leaving no room for significant achievements. It's the perfect way to fill your days with the illusion of effort without the burden of results. The world will adjust to your pace, and if it doesn't, at least you'll be well-rested and relaxed.

The Delay Dynamo

Delay Dynamo is all about timing — or the lack thereof. You can delay anything — chores, decisions, personal growth, whatever you want, you name it. Case in point: I've delayed writing this book for over a decade. Quite the achievement, don't you think? I mean, I wasn't really expecting this level of procrastination from myself. And from my very own painstakingly honed experience, I know this crap well enough, so trust me. If it worked for me, it would work one hundred percent for you as well.

So, I was saying, delay every task, every resolution, and every action with the grace of a seasoned procrastinator. Delaying is another form of art that requires a deep appreciation for the slow, sweet passage of time. It's about revelling in the beauty in deferment, the elegance in elongation. Why do today what you can put off until the next millennium? It is as simple as that.

This technique demands an innate ability to delay everything and is particularly effective when combined with a total lack of organization. By everything, we mean everything. Got an email? Perfect, reply in a week. Got a project? Excellent, start next month. By keeping no track of deadlines or responsibilities, you ensure that tasks are cheerfully forgotten and abandoned in the abyss of good intentions.

Embracing this delay-centric lifestyle means embracing a life of perpetual waiting. Waiting for the perfect moment, which, let's be honest, never arrives. Waiting for inspiration, which is always just out of reach. Waiting for the stars to align, which they resolutely refuse to do. Keep delaying, and you'll never have to face the discomfort of actually accomplishing anything.

Make it a lifestyle choice. The beauty of it is in the thrill of last-minute scrambles and the adrenaline rush of narrowly avoiding disaster. Life is more exciting when everything hangs by a thread. This strategy not only keeps stress at bay but also ensures you have a constant stream of tasks awaiting you, keeping life interesting and perpetually chaotic. There's no need to hurry when you can simply wait. And wait. And wait. Eventually, the task will either become irrelevant or someone else will do it for you. Either way, you win.

The Last-Minute Maverick

Some folks think pressure is bad, but you know that pressure makes diamonds. So why waste time meticulously planning and executing tasks when you can savour the electrifying rush of doing everything at the eleventh hour? The thrill of racing against the clock is unparalleled. Procrastination isn't just about avoiding work; it is a high-octane activity.

Imagine the heart-pounding excitement of starting a project mere hours before it's due. The sheer terror of watching the clock tick down as you frantically try to piece together something halfway decent. The Last-Minute Maverick thrives on the pressure of impending deadlines, believing that true genius only emerges under extreme duress.

This lifestyle demands a delicate balance of procrastination and panic, ensuring you only start working when the pressure is unbearable. This also guarantees that you'll never have to worry about over-preparing or delivering anything of high quality.

However, the reality is far less glamorous. Rushed work is usually subpar, filled with errors, and lacking in depth. But that's the beauty of it! By consistently working at the last minute, you guarantee a continuous cycle of stress, mediocrity, and disappointment. It's a surefire path to achieving that sense of failure for which we're all striving.

It's a high-stakes game of beat-the-clock, and you wouldn't have it any other way. Plus, if it turns out poorly, you can always blame the lack of time. It's like living on the edge, flirting with disaster. The chaos, the panic, the sense of impending doom — it's all part of the exhilarating experience.

The Lazy Lion

Why strive for excellence when you can excel at doing nothing? The Lazy Lion epitomizes lethargy, majestically sprawled out and perfecting the art of minimal effort. Lions, those regal powerhouses, spend up to 20 hours a day in the horizontal position. If it's good enough for the jungle's royalty, it's certainly good enough for you. Embracing laziness isn't a sign of being unproductive; it's a testament to prioritizing self-care. Why hustle when you can lounge? Why exert when you can relax? Being lazy is about adopting a lifestyle of maximum relaxation with minimal effort. Your body and mind will shower you with gratitude for the abundant rest.

Devote your days to napping, binge-watching TV shows, and mastering the delicate balance of doing absolutely nothing. Productivity is for those poor souls who haven't yet discovered the luxury of extended rest and relaxation. Place rest on a pedestal above all else. This approach champions your inner couch potato, discarding any delusions of effort or ambition. As we delved into great detail in *Chapter 5 – Exercise: How to Avoid It*, laziness is not a shortcoming; it's a philosophy. It's about watching the world zoom by as you bask in the splendour of idleness. The more you rest, the less you do, and the closer you come to becoming a procrastination virtuoso. The ultimate aim is to become so adept at being lazy that you forget what productivity even feels like.

Rest reigns supreme, after all, and should you ever feel the itch to accomplish something, just remind yourself of the critical importance of energy conservation. Lounge with pride, knowing you've reached the zenith of procrastination. Remember, a well-rested procrastinator is a joyful procrastinator. And who can argue with happiness?

The Productivity Pariah

Productivity is a social construct designed to keep you from enjoying life. The Productivity Pariah knows this all too well and shuns any attempt to be productive. Shunning productivity means actively avoiding anything that smacks of achievement. It's about scrolling endlessly on social media, binge-watching TV shows, and finding new ways to waste time. Please note that true happiness lies not in doing but in not doing. This technique involves a steadfast refusal to engage in any activity that could be considered remotely useful.

Ditch those to-do lists, planners, and productivity apps. Who needs structure when you can revel in chaos and spontaneity? Fill your hours with joyful activities like aimless social media scrolling or the meticulous organization of your refrigerator one more time. After all, what's the point of being productive if it means giving up your precious freedom and happiness?

Productivity is for the unenlightened masses who cling to notions like progress and achievement. But not you — you're far too wise for that nonsense. Plus, it is overrated, isn't it? So, reject the hustle culture and let others burn out while you glide through life with minimal effort. As others strive for self-improvement, you should be perfecting your skills in doing nothing. While they're setting goals, you should be setting your sights on another episode of your favourite show. Spend hours contemplating the meaning of life, watching clouds drift by from left to right, or refining your expertise in idleness.

Sure, productivity might fuel the world, but your lack of it fuels your peace of mind. Take pride in your inactivity.

Revel in your resistance. Bask in the serenity that comes from shunning the rat race and settling into a life of deliberate unproductiveness. It's liberating to know you've opted out of society's relentless pursuit of productivity. The less you produce, the less you have to worry about maintaining any pesky standards of achievement.

The Efficiency Evasion

Efficiency is the enemy of procrastination. The Efficiency Evasion technique is about actively avoiding any methods or strategies that could make you more efficient. This includes rejecting any time management tools that you may accidentally be using, ignoring productivity hacks that you might have learned along the way, and generally doing everything the hard way.

Imagine a world where you never have to worry about being efficient, where you can take as long as you like to complete any task, free from the oppressive pressure of optimization. This approach is about embracing inefficiency in all its forms, ensuring that you remain blissfully unproductive.

Efficiency is a trap designed to lure you into the quicksand of productivity and to suck the joy out of life. Evade it at all costs. To evade this snare, ensure that you never take the shortest, most effective route to completing a task. Instead, complicate every process, introduce unnecessary steps, and make every effort to be as inefficient as possible.

Take the scenic route, opt for the long-winded solution, and always ensure that your methods are as convoluted as possible. Sometimes, use outdated methods as well for an added touch of inefficiency. If you need to send an email, draft it multiple times, each one worse than the last. If you're cleaning your house, clean one square inch at a time, ensuring you get distracted frequently. Efficiency evasion is about creating elaborate and convoluted ways to achieve the simplest of tasks, thereby guaranteeing that you never actually finish anything.

Efficiency is a slippery slope, leading to more work. The more efficient you are, the more tasks you'll be assigned. Thus, the Efficiency Evasion tactic is crucial. Evade efficiency at all costs. By doing so, you create the illusion of effort without actually achieving much. The true procrastinator knows that doing less is the key to happiness. Evading efficiency means you have more time to do the things you love. Remember, the goal is not to accomplish tasks quickly but to stretch them out and savour the leisurely journey.

The Procrastination Pro

Finally, become a true virtuoso in the Symphony of Procrastination by mastering all the techniques detailed above. Mastering procrastination isn't just about knowing when to delay and for how long; it's about crafting the most creative and convincing excuses for putting things off. It's about deferring everything until tomorrow, dancing around deadlines, inventing excuses, plodding through tasks at a snail's pace, and shunning productivity as if it's a contagious disease. It's about delaying everything, doing things at the last possible moment, embracing laziness, dodging efficiency, and perfecting the intricate art of procrastination.

As a Procrastination Pro, you'll seamlessly weave together all these strategies into a magnificent tapestry of delay and avoidance. You'll develop an almost magical ability to conjure up reasons for inaction and perfect the art of starting tasks with no intention of ever finishing them. Your ultimate goal is to become so skilled at procrastination that it becomes second nature — an integral part of your very identity.

Procrastination allows you to live a life entirely on your terms, unburdened by the pesky constraints of deadlines and expectations. You've honed your skills and perfected your techniques, and now you're ready to impart your wisdom to others. Let's be clear: this isn't about being lazy — it's about mastering the delicate craft of postponement. It's about doing just enough to keep everything from completely falling apart while never doing more than the bare minimum.

For example, develop an impressive portfolio of unfinished projects. Revel in the chaos, the stress, and the never-ending cycle of putting things off. Strive to become the person who has turned procrastination into an art form, a lifestyle, a creed. Congratulations, you're headed straight for the pinnacle of perpetual misery!

Practical Exercises

To help you master these techniques, here are some practical exercises:

1. *Calendar Clash*: Double-book your schedule, then cancel both appointments.

2. *List Limbo*: Make a to-do list, then lose it. Repeatedly.

3. *Coffee Confusion*: Spend an hour making the perfect cup of coffee. Drink it slowly.

4. *Email Escapism*: Read old emails. All of them.

5. *Social Media Spiral*: Get lost in social media. Research cat memes for hours.

6. *Perfectionist Pitfall*: Start a project. Abandon it because it's not perfect.

7. *Netflix Nirvana*: Watch an entire series. Tell yourself it's for research.

8. *Procrastination Procrastination*: Plan to procrastinate, then procrastinate on that.

9. *Turtle Tasking*: Complete one tiny task at an excruciatingly slow pace.

10. *Reflection Ritual*: Reflect on your procrastination skills. Think about improving them tomorrow.

And there you have it, the epitome of procrastination mastery! You've now been equipped with the most refined techniques for dodging productivity like a pro. As you wade through the glorious mess of your postponed tasks and endless excuses, remember: why do today what you can skilfully delay until tomorrow? Embrace the chaos, cherish your expertly crafted inefficiency, and let your inner procrastinator shine. After all, if life's a race, you've already perfected the art of falling behind with style. Cheers to your unproductive future!

***

"Finding Your Way Out of the Dark"

Congratulations! If you've made it this far without tossing this book into the nearest fireplace or dramatically tearing out its pages in a fit of existential despair, you truly are a champion of suffering. You have navigated through the treacherous waters of self-sabotage with the finesse of a seasoned captain steering the Titanic straight into an iceberg. But fear not, dear reader, for all journeys, no matter how misguided, must come to an end. And so, we arrive at our conclusion, which, in keeping with the spirit of this guide, offers no miraculous transformations or fairy-tale endings. Instead, it's a celebration of the deliciously dark humour that has accompanied us on this twisted path.

Throughout this guide, you've mastered the art of transforming everyday annoyances into existential catastrophes. You've learned to bottle up emotions with the proficiency of a seasoned winemaker, ensuring that when they finally uncork, it'll be a vintage display of spectacular emotional pyrotechnics. You've surrounded yourselves with individuals so toxic that they could qualify as hazardous waste, ensuring your social interactions are as draining as a marathon. You've learned how to sacrifice sleep for anxiety, how to transform your workplace into a soul-sucking vortex, and, perhaps most importantly, how to avoid exercise.

But let's be real — while this guide has explored the art of descending into depression with a tongue-in-cheek ferocity, the true lesson lies in the absurdity of it all. By exaggerating the ways we make our lives harder, we find a backdoor into understanding how we might make them a bit easier or at least more bearable. The goal here was never really to encourage true misery. Life, with its endless challenges and pitfalls, sometimes feels like a dark comedy scripted by a particularly sadistic writer. Yet, it is in this recognition that a strange kind of comfort can be found — the realization that if we're all stumbling through the darkness, perhaps we're not as alone as we thought.

If this guide has taught you anything, it's that there is a peculiar joy to be found in embracing the chaos of life. It's not about seeking out suffering but about acknowledging that pain, like laughter, is a fundamental part of the human experience. So why not approach it with a bit of humour? Why not laugh at the cosmic joke that is existence rather than letting it crush you?

As you close this book, consider this: the light at the end of the tunnel might not always be visible, but that doesn't mean you can't light a torch and dance in the shadows. Life will throw curveballs, drench you in the rain, and occasionally serve you a cocktail of catastrophes. But in these moments, there's an opportunity to write your own script, one that includes laughter amidst the tears and strength in the face of adversity.

Remember, the guide to going into depression is also a map for finding your way out. Each sarcastic tip, each ludicrous piece of advice, serves as a reminder of what not to do if you want to find a semblance of peace. So, take this journey with a grain of salt and a generous helping of humour. Use it not as a manual for misery but as a light-hearted lamp to guide you through the darker times.

In conclusion, *"An Epic Guide to Go into Depression"* is not just a book; it's a companion for those moments when life seems a bit too overwhelming. It's a reminder that sometimes, the best way to deal with life's absurdities is to laugh at them — because, at the end of the day, the ability to find humour in the darkness is perhaps the most powerful weapon we have.

So go forth, armed with your new-found knowledge of despair, and use it to do the exact opposite. Find joy in the little things, cherish the good moments, and when the going gets tough, remember that even the darkest clouds can have a silver lining — if you're willing to look for it. After all, if life insists on being a tragicomedy, you might as well get a few good laughs in. Cheers!

***

Acknowledgments

To my readers: I am profoundly grateful for the opportunity to make a difference in your lives. Your support means the world to me, and even if just one person reads this, I am inspired to keep going for that one person.

To my wonderful wife, Glory: Your encouragement is invaluable, and your unwavering support in my life is nothing short of a miracle. I am deeply thankful for your belief in me, for patiently reading my manuscript, and for always standing by my side.

To my beloved children, Megan and David: Though you are too young to fully understand this, you are my inspiration. I love you more than words can express.

To my parents: Without your love and guidance, I would not be here today. Your support has been the foundation upon which I've built my journey.

To my in-laws: Thank you for loving me and embracing me into your family. Your warmth and kindness have meant so much to me.

To my brother, Anugrah: I have always looked up to you, and your presence has been a guiding light in my life.

To my mentor, Mr. Neeraj Chandhok: Your guidance throughout my college days and during the publication journey of this book has been crucial. Thank you for your wisdom and support.

To my friend, Mayuri Ganesh Khode: Your meticulous proofreading, editing, and invaluable feedback have played a significant role in shaping this book. Thank you for your dedication and insight. I am glad to have you as someone who I can always go back to and blame it all for those tiny mistakes, if any.

To my friends, Ujjwal Minz and Joy Aniket Ekka: Your silent presence during my hardest depressive times has been a source of great comfort. Though I may not have spoken about it, your support — whether through encouragement, understanding, or just being there for me on weekends — kept me motivated and engaged.

To all my friends who believed in me and my struggle: Your faith and support never wavered, and you never gave up on me.

To my Publisher, Notion Press: Thank you for giving me the opportunity to turn my dreams into reality. Your support has been instrumental in bringing this book to life.

To all the support staff at Notion Press: Your assistance with logistics, formatting, and various tasks related to the publication process has been invaluable. Thank you for your hard work and dedication.

Last but not least, to everyone who pushed me into a situation where writing this book was my only option: Your influence has driven me to create something meaningful not just for me but for everyone out there facing the same heat of life, and for that, I am forever grateful.

***